GRAPHS, MAPS, TREES

GRAPHS, MAPS, TREES

Abstract Models for a Literary History

FRANCO MORETTI

VERSO

London • New York

First published by Verso 2005
This paperback edition published by Verso 2007
© Franco Moretti 2005, 2007

1 3 5 7 9 10 8 6 4 2

Verso
UK: 6 Meard Street, London W1F 0EG
USA: 388 Atlantic Ave, Brooklyn, NY 11217
www.versobooks.com

Verso is the imprint of New Left Books

ISBN–13: 978–1–84467–185–4

British Library Cataloguing in Publication Data
A catalogue record for this book is available from the British Library

Library of Congress Cataloging-in-Publication Data
A catalog record for this book is available from the Library of Congress

Printed in the United States

CONTENTS

LIST OF FIGURES

Graphs, maps, trees

> A man who wants the truth becomes a scientist; a man who wants to give free play to his subjectivity may become a writer; but what should a man do who wants something in between?
>
> Robert Musil, *The Man without Qualities*

The title of this short book deserves a few words of explanation. To begin with, this is an essay on literary history: literature, the old territory (more or less), unlike the drift towards other discourses so typical of recent years. But within that old territory, a new object of study: instead of concrete, individual works, a trio of artificial constructs—graphs, maps, and trees—in which the reality of the text undergoes a process of deliberate reduction and abstraction. 'Distant reading', I have once called this type of approach;[1] where distance is however not an obstacle, but *a specific form of knowledge*: fewer elements, hence a sharper sense of their overall interconnection. Shapes, relations, structures. Forms. Models.

From texts to models, then; and models drawn from three disciplines with which literary studies have had little or no interaction: graphs

---

[1] 'Conjectures on World Literature', *New Left Review* I, Jan–Feb 2000.

from quantitative history, maps from geography, and trees from evolutionary theory. The distant reason for these choices lies in my Marxist formation, which was profoundly influenced by Galvano DellaVolpe, and entailed therefore (in principle, if not always in practice) a great respect for the scientific spirit. And so, while recent literary theory was turning for inspiration towards French and German metaphysics, I kept thinking that there was actually much more to be learned from the natural and the social sciences. This book is a result of that conviction, and also, in its small way, an attempt to open a new front of discussion.

Finally, these three models are indeed, as the subtitle intimates, abstract. But their consequences are on the other hand extremely concrete: graphs, maps, and trees place the literary field literally in front of our eyes—and show us how little we still know about it. It is a double lesson, of humility and euphoria at the same time: humility for what literary history has accomplished so far (not enough), and euphoria for what still remains to be done (a lot). Here, the methodology of the book reveals its pragmatic ambition: for me, abstraction is not an end in itself, but a way to widen the domain of the literary historian, and enrich its internal problematic. How this may be done, is what I will try to explain.[2]

[2] This book was first imagined at the Wissenschaftskolleg in Berlin, and presented in an early version as the Beckman Lectures at Berkeley, and then elsewhere. My thanks to the many people who have helped me to clarify my ideas, and to Matt Jockers, who patiently taught me how to improve the book's visual side.

Graphs

Before the advent of the Annales, Krzysztof Pomian once wrote,

> the gaze of the historian [was directed] towards extraordinary events
> . . . historians resembled collectors: both gathered only rare and curi-
> ous objects, disregarding whatever looked banal, everyday, normal . . .
> History was an idiographic discipline, having as its object that which
> does not repeat itself.[1]

History *was* . . . Pomian speaks in the past tense here, as is probably
accurate in the case of social history, but certainly not for its literary
counterpart, where the collector of rare and curious works, that do
not repeat themselves, exceptional—and which close reading makes
even more exceptional, by emphasizing the uniqueness of exactly *this*
word and *this* sentence here—is still by far the dominant figure. But
what would happen if literary historians, too, decided to 'shift their
gaze' (Pomian again) 'from the extraordinary to the everyday, from
exceptional events to the large mass of facts'? What literature would
we find, in 'the large mass of facts'?

All questions that occurred to me some years ago, when the study
of national bibliographies made me realize what a minimal fraction

[1] Krzysztof Pomian, 'L'histoire des structures', in Jacques Le Goff, Roger Chartier,
Jacques Revel, eds, *La nouvelle histoire*, Paris 1978, pp. 115–16.

of the literary field we all work on: a canon of two hundred novels, for instance, sounds very large for nineteenth-century Britain (and *is* much larger than the current one), but is still less than one per cent of the novels that were actually published: twenty thousand, thirty, more, no one really knows—and close reading won't help here, a novel a day every day of the year would take a century or so . . . And it's not even a matter of time, but of method: a field this large cannot be understood by stitching together separate bits of knowledge about individual cases, because it *isn't* a sum of individual cases: it's a collective system, that should be grasped as such, as a whole—and the graphs that follow are one way to begin doing this. Or as Fernand Braudel put it in the lecture on history he gave to his companions in the German prison camp near Lübeck:

> An incredible number of dice, always rolling, dominate and determine each individual existence: uncertainty, then, in the realm of individual history; but in that of collective history . . . simplicity and consistency. History is indeed 'a poor little conjectural science' when it selects individuals as its objects . . . but much more rational in its procedures and results, when it examines groups and repetitions.[2]

A more rational literary history. That is the idea.

I

The quantitative approach to literature can take several different forms—from computational stylistics to thematic databases, book history, and more. For reasons of space, I will here limit myself to book history, building on work originally done by McBurney, Beasley, Raven, Garside and Block for Britain; Angus, Mylne and Frautschi for France; Zwicker for Japan; Petersen for Denmark; Ragone for Italy;

[2] Fernand Braudel, 'L'histoire, mesure du monde', in *Les écrits de Fernand Braudel*, vol. II, Paris 1997.

Martí-Lopez and Santana for Spain; Joshi for India; and Griswold for Nigeria. And I mention these names right away because quantitative work is truly *cooperation*: not only in the pragmatic sense that it takes forever to gather the data, but because such data are ideally independent from any individual researcher, and can thus be shared by others, and combined in more than one way. Figure 1 (overleaf), which charts the take-off of the novel in Britain, Japan, Italy, Spain and Nigeria, is a case in point. See how similar those shapes are: five countries, three continents, over two centuries apart, and it's really the same pattern, the same old metaphor of the 'rise' of the novel come alive: in twenty years or so (in Britain, 1720–40; Japan, 1745–65; Italy, 1820–40; Spain, 1845 to early 1860s; Nigeria, 1965–80), the graph leaps from five–ten new titles per year, which means one new novel every month or two, to one new novel *per week*. And at this point, the horizon of novel-reading changes. As long as only a handful of new titles are published each year, I mean, novels remain unreliable products, that disappear for long stretches of time, and cannot really command the loyalty of the reading public; they are commodities, yes—but commodities still waiting for a fully developed market. A new novel per week, by contrast, is already the great capitalist oxymoron of the *regular novelty*: the unexpected that is produced with such efficiency and punctuality that readers become unable to do without it. The novel 'becomes a necessity of life', to paraphrase the title of a book by William Gilmore-Lehne, and the jeremiads that immediately multiply around it—novels make readers lazy, stupid, dissolute, insane, insubordinate: exactly like films two centuries later—are the clearest sign of its symbolic triumph.

II

The rise of the novel, then; or, better, *one* rise in a history which had begun many centuries earlier, and will go through several other accelerations, as emerges quite clearly from the data on the publication

FIGURE 1: *The rise of the novel, 18th to 20th century*

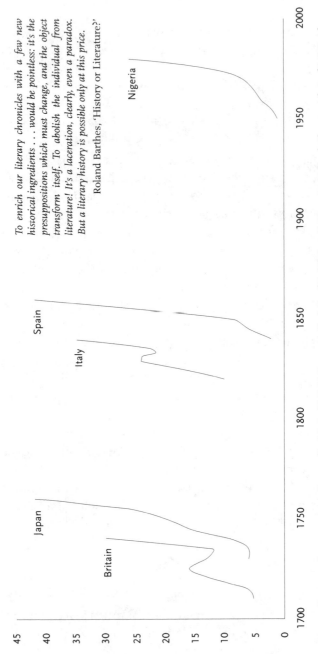

To enrich our literary chronicles with a few new historical ingredients . . . would be pointless: it's the presuppositions which must change, and the object transform itself. To abolish the individual from literature! It's a laceration, clearly, even a paradox. But a literary history is possible only at this price.

Roland Barthes, 'History or Literature?'

New novels per year, by 5-year average. Sources: For Britain: W. H. McBurney, *A Check List of English Prose Fiction, 1700–39*, Cambridge, MA 1960, and J. C. Beasley, *The Novels of the 1740s*, Athens, GA 1982; both partly revised by James Raven, *British Fiction 1750–70: A Chronological Check-List of Prose Fiction Printed in Britain and Ireland*, London 1987. For Japan: Jonathan Zwicker, 'Il lungo Ottocento del romanzo giapponese', in *Il romanzo*, vol. III, *Storia e geografia*, Torino 2002. For Italy: Giovanni Ragone, 'Italia 1815–70', in *Il romanzo*, vol. III. For Spain: Elisa Martí-López and Mario Santana, 'Spagna 1843–1900'. *Il romanzo*, vol. III. For Nigeria: Wendy Griswold, 'Nigeria 1950–2000', *Il romanzo*, vol. III.

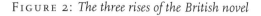

FIGURE 2: *The three rises of the British novel*

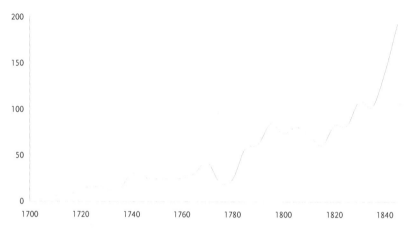

New novels per year, by 5-year average. Sources: McBurney, *Check List of English Prose Fiction, 1700–39*; Beasley, *The Novels of the 1740s*; Raven, *British Fiction 1750–70*; Peter Garside, James Raven and Rainer Schöwerling, eds, *The English Novel 1770–1829*, 2 vols, Oxford 2000; Andrew Block, *The English Novel, 1740–1850*, London 1961.

of new novels in Britain between 1710 and 1850 (figure 2). Here, three phases seem to stand out, each subdivided into a first period of rapid growth and a second one of stabilization, and each modifying in a specific way the social role of the novel. The first phase, from 1720 to around 1770, is the one discussed above: a leap in 1720–40, and a consolidation in the following decades. In the second phase, which runs from 1770 to around 1820, the further increase in the number of new titles induces for its part a drastic reorientation of audiences towards the present. Up to then, I mean, the 'extensive' reading so typical of the novel—reading many texts once and super-ficially, rather than a few texts often and intensely—would easily outgrow the yearly output of titles, forcing readers to turn to the past for (much of) their entertainment: all sorts of reprints and abridge-ments of eighteenth-century bestsellers, British as well as foreign, plus the old, and even the few ancient classics of the genre. But as the total of new novels doubles, compared to the previous phase—80 in 1788; 91 in 1796; 111 in 1808—the popularity of old books suddenly collapses, and novelistic audiences turn resolutely (and irreversibly) towards the current season.[3]

The third phase, which begins around 1820, and which unfortunately I can only follow for the first thirty years, is the one in which the *internal composition* of the market changes. So far, the typical reader of novels had been a 'generalist'—someone 'who reads absolutely anything, at random', as Thibaudet was to write with a touch of contempt in *Le liseur de romans*.[4] Now, however, the growth of the market creates all sorts of niches for 'specialist' readers and genres (nautical tales, sporting novels, school stories, *mystères*): the books aimed at urban workers in the second quarter of the nineteenth century, or at boys, and then girls, in the following generation, are simply the most visible instances of this larger process, which culminates at the turn of the century in the super-niches of detective fiction and then science fiction.

Abstract models for literary history . . . and we certainly have abstraction here: *Pamela, The Monk, The Wild Irish Girl, Persuasion, Oliver Twist*—where are they? five tiny dots in the graph of figure 2, indistinguishable from all others. But graphs are not really *models*; they are not simplified, intuitive versions of a theoretical structure in the way maps and (especially) evolutionary trees will be in the next two chapters.

---

[3] 'In Italy,' writes Giovanni Ragone, 'in the first twenty years of the nineteenth century virtually all the bestsellers of the previous century disappear', 'Italia 1815–1870', in *Il romanzo*, vol. III, pp. 343–54. A similar shift seems to occur in France, where, however, the caesura of the revolution offers a very strong alternative explanation. The 'pastness of the past' is of course the key message of the two genres—gothic, and then historical novels—most responsible for the turn towards the present.

[4] Albert Thibaudet, *Il lettore di romanzi* [1925], Napoli 2000, p. 49.

Quantitative research provides a type of data which is ideally independent of interpretations, I said earlier, and that is of course also its limit: it provides *data*, not interpretation. That figure 2 shows a first 'rise' (when the novel becomes a necessity of life), and then a second (the shift from the past to the present), and then a third (the multiplication of market niches), seems to me a good account of the data, but is certainly far from inevitable. Quantitative data can tell us when Britain produced one new novel per month, or week, or day, or hour for that matter, but where the significant turning points lie along the continuum—and why—is something that must be decided on a different basis.

III

A—multiple—rise of the novel. But with an interesting twist, which is particularly visible in the Japanese case of figure 3 (overleaf): after the rise from one novel per month in the mid-1740s to one per week twenty years later (and even more in the following years: between 1750 and 1820, in fact, many more novels are published in Japan than in Britain; a fact which deserves a good explanation!)—several equally rapid downturns occur in 1780–90, the 1810s to the 1830s, and in 1860–70. The fall of the novel. And the reason behind the downturns seems to be always the same: politics—a direct, virulent censorship during the Kansei and Tempo periods, and an indirect influence in the years leading up to the Meiji Restoration, when there was no specific repression of the book trade, and the crisis was thus probably due to a more general dissonance between the rhythm of political crises and the writing of novels. It's the same in Denmark during the Napoleonic wars (figure 4, overleaf), or in France and Italy (better, Milan) in comparable situations (figure 5, overleaf): after 1789, the publication of French novels drops about 80 per cent; after the first Risorgimento war, the Milanese downturn is around 90 per cent, with only 3 novels published in the course of 1849, against 43 in 1842.

FIGURE 3: *The fall of the novel: Japan*

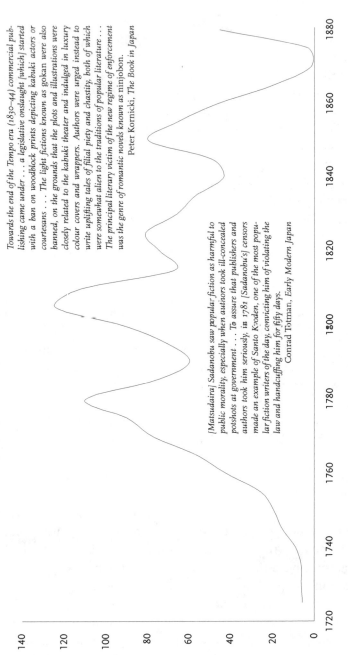

Towards the end of the Tempo era (1830–44) commercial pub-
lishing came under . . . a legislative onslaught [which] started
with a ban on woodblock prints depicting kabuki actors or
courtesans . . . The light fictions known as gokan were also
banned, on the grounds that the plots and illustrations were
closely related to the kabuki theater and indulged in luxury
colour covers and wrappers. Authors were urged instead to
write uplifting tales of filial piety and chastity, both of which
were somewhat alien to the traditions of popular literature . . .
The principal literary victim of the new regime of enforcement
was the genre of romantic novels known as ninjobon.

Peter Kornicki, *The Book in Japan*

[Matsudaira] Sadanobu saw popular fiction as harmful to
public morality, especially when authors took ill-concealed
potshots at government . . . To assure that publishers and
authors took him seriously, in 1791 [Sadanobu's] censors
made an example of Santo Kyoden, one of the most popular fiction writers of the day, convicting him of violating the
law and handcuffing him for fifty days.

Conrad Totman, *Early Modern Japan*

New novels per year, by 5-year average. Source: Jonathan Zwicker, 'Il lungo Ottocento del romanzo giapponese', in *Il romanzo*, vol. III.
See also Totman, *Early Modern Japan*, Berkeley 1993; Kornicki, *The Book in Japan*, Leiden 1998.

FIGURE 4: *The fall of the novel: Denmark*

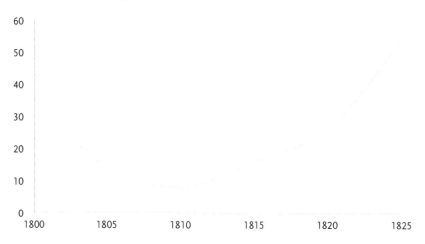

New novels per year, by 5-year average. Source: Erland Munch-Petersen, *Die Übersetzungsliteratur als Unterhaltung des romantischen Lesers*, Wiesbaden 1991.

FIGURE 5: *The fall of the novel: France, Italy*

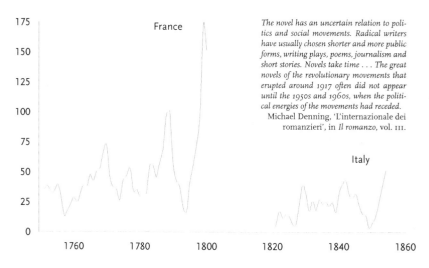

The novel has an uncertain relation to politics and social movements. Radical writers have usually chosen shorter and more public forms, writing plays, poems, journalism and short stories. Novels take time . . . The great novels of the revolutionary movements that erupted around 1917 often did not appear until the 1950s and 1960s, when the political energies of the movements had receded.

Michael Denning, 'L'internazionale dei romanzieri', in *Il romanzo*, vol. III.

New novels per year. Sources: For France: Angus Martin, Vivienne G. Mylne and Richard Frautschi, eds, *Bibliographie du genre romanesque français 1751–1800*, Paris 1977. For Milan: Giovanni Ragone, 'Italia 1815–70', in *Il romanzo*, vol. III, and *Catalogo dei libri italiani dell'Ottocento*, Milano 1991.

FIGURE 6: *Book imports into India*

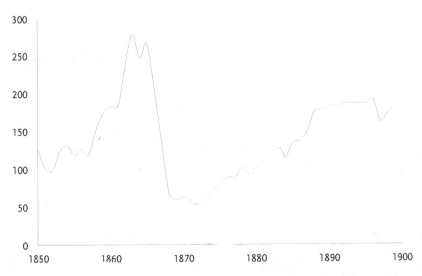

Thousands of pounds sterling. Source: Priya Joshi, *In Another Country: Colonialism, Culture, and the English Novel in India*, New York 2002.

The only exception I know to this pattern is the import of British books into India charted by Priya Joshi (figure 6), which rises sharply after the 1857 rebellion; but as Joshi points out, the logic of a colonial relationship is reversed, and the peak is a sign of Britain suddenly accelerating the pace of symbolic hegemony; then, once the crisis is over, the flow returns to its pre-1857 levels.

IV

An antipathy between politics and the novel. Still, it would be odd if *all* crises in novelistic production had a political origin: the French downturn of the 1790s was sharp, true, but there had been others in the 1750s and 1770s—as there had been in Britain, for that matter, notwithstanding its greater institutional stability. The American and the Napoleonic wars may well be behind the slumps of 1775–83 and 1810–17 (which are clearly visible in figure 2), write Raven and Garside in their splendid bibliographic studies; but then they add to the political factor 'a decade of poorly produced novels', 'reprints', the possible 'greater relative popularity . . . of other fictional forms', 'a backlash against low fiction', the high cost of paper . . .[5] And as possible causes multiply, one wonders: what are we trying to explain here—two *unrelated individual events*, or two moments *in a recurring pattern of ups and downs?* Because if the downturns are individual events, then looking for individual causes (Napoleon, reprints, the cost of paper, whatever) makes perfect sense; but if they are parts of a pattern, then what we must explain is *the pattern as a whole*, not just one of its phases.

The whole pattern; or, as some historians would say, the whole cycle: 'An increasingly clear idea has emerged . . . of the multiplicity of time', writes Braudel in the essay on *longue durée*:

> Traditional history, with its concern for the short time span, for the individual and the event, has long accustomed us to the headlong, dramatic, breathless rush of its narrative . . . The new economic and social history puts cyclical movement in the forefront of its research . . . large sections of the past, ten, twenty, fifty years at a stretch . . . Far beyond this . . . we find a history capable of traversing even greater distances . . . to be measured in centuries . . . the long, even the very long time span, the *longue durée*.[6]

---

[5] James Raven, 'Historical Introduction: the Novel Comes of Age', and Peter Garside, 'The English Novel in the Romantic Era: Consolidation and Dispersal', in Peter Garside, James Raven and Rainer Schöwerling, eds, *The English Novel 1770–1829*, 2 vols, Oxford 2000; vol. i, p. 27, and vol. ii, p. 44.

[6] Fernand Braudel, 'History and the Social Sciences. The *longue durée*', in *On History*, Chicago 1980, p. 27. The first extended treatment of economic cycles was of course Nikolai Kondratiev's *The Long Wave Cycle*, written between 1922 and 1928.

Event, cycle, *longue durée*: three time frames which have fared very unevenly in literary studies. Most critics are perfectly at ease with the first one, the circumscribed domain of the event and of the individual case; most theorists are at home at the opposite end of the temporal spectrum, in the very long span of nearly unchanging structures. But the middle level has remained somewhat unexplored by literary historians; and it's not even that we don't work within that time frame, it's that we haven't yet fully understood its specificity: the fact, I mean, that cycles constitute *temporary structures within the historical flow*. That is, after all, the hidden logic behind Braudel's tripartition: the short span is all flow and no structure, the *longue durée* all structure and no flow, and cycles are the—unstable—border country between them. Structures, because they introduce repetition in history, and hence regularity, order, pattern; and temporary, because they're short (ten, twenty, fifty years, this depends on the theory).

Now, 'temporary structures' is also a good definition for—genres: morphological arrangements that *last* in time, but always only for *some* time. Janus-like creatures, with one face turned to history and the other to form, genres are thus the true protagonists of this middle layer of literary history—this more 'rational' layer where flow and form meet. It's the regularity of figures 7 and 8 (overleaf), with their three waves of epistolary novels from 1760 to 1790, and then gothic novels from 1790 to 1815, and then historical novels from 1815 to the 1840s. Each wave produces more or less the same number of novels per year, and lasts the same 25–30 years, and each also rises only after the previous wave has begun to ebb away (see how the up- and downward trends intersect around 1790 and 1815). 'The new form makes its appearance to replace an old form that has outlived its artistic usefulness', writes Shklovsky, and the decline of a ruling genre seems indeed here to be the necessary precondition for its successor's takeoff. Which may explain those odd 'latency periods' in the early history of genres: *Pamela* is published in 1740, and *The Castle of Otranto* in 1764, but very few epistolary or gothic novels are written until 1760

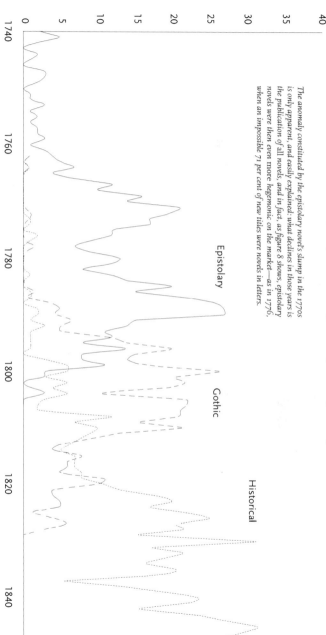

FIGURE 7: *British hegemonic forms, 1760–1850*

The anomaly constituted by the epistolary novel's slump in the 1770s is only apparent, and easily explained: what declines in those years is the publication of all novels, and in fact, as figure 8 shows, epistolary novels were then even more hegemonic on the market—as in 1776, when an impossible 71 per cent of new titles were novels in letters.

Epistolary

Gothic

Historical

New novels per year. Sources: For the epistolary novel: James Raven, 'Gran Bretagna 1750–1830', in *Il romanzo*, vol. III, pp. 311–12. For the gothic novel: Maurice Lévy, *Le roman 'gothique' anglais*, Paris 1995. For the historical novel, I have taken as the basis the checklist provided by Rainer Schöwerling ('Sir Walter Scott and the Tradition of the Historical Novel before 1814', in Uwe Böker, Manfred Markus, Rainer Schöwerling, eds, *The Living Middle Ages*, Stuttgart 1989), and subtracted those texts that also appear in Lévy's bibliography of the gothic; for the later period, I have also used Block, *The English Novel, 1740–1850*.

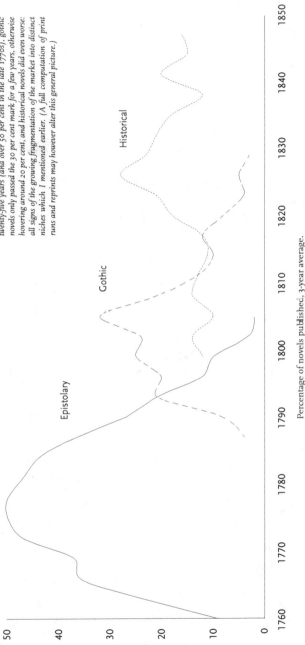

FIGURE 8: *Market quotas of British hegemonic forms, 1760–1850*

All works of art, and not only parodies, are created either as a parallel or an antithesis to some model. The new form makes its appearance not in order to express a new content, but rather to replace an old form that has already outlived its artistic usefulness.

Viktor Shklovsky, *A Theory of Prose*

As more and more novels are published every year, the hegemony of a single genre tends to become less and less absolute: whereas epistolary novels amounted to 30 per cent or more of the market for twenty-five years (and over 50 per cent in the late 1770s), gothic novels only passed the 30 per cent mark for a few years, otherwise hovering around 20 per cent, and historical novels did even worse: all signs of the growing fragmentation of the market into distinct niches which I mentioned earlier. (A full computation of print runs and reprints may however alter this general picture.)

Epistolary

Gothic

Historical

Percentage of novels published, 3-year average.

and 1790 respectively. Why the lag? Almost certainly, because as long
as a hegemonic form has not lost its 'artistic usefulness', there is not
much that a rival form can do: there can always be an exceptional
text, yes, but the exception *will not change the system*. It's only when
Ptolemaic astronomy begins to generate one 'monstrosity' after
another, writes Kuhn in *The Structure of Scientific Revolutions*, that
'the time comes to give a competitor a chance'—and the same is true
here: a historical novel written in 1800, such as *Castle Rackrent* (or
in 1805, like *Waverley*'s abandoned first draft) simply didn't have the
incredible opportunity to reshape the literary field that the collapse of
the gothic offered *Waverley* in 1814.[7]

V

From individual cases to series; from series to cycles, and then to
genres as their morphological embodiment. And these three genres

---

[7] A few more words on why a form loses its 'artistic usefulness' and disappears.
For Shklovsky, the reason is the purely inner dialectic of art, which begins in creative estrangement, and ends in stale automatism: 'Each art form travels down
the inevitable road from birth to death; from seeing and sensory perception,
when every detail in the object is savoured and relished, to mere recognition,
when form becomes a dull epigone which our senses register mechanically, a
piece of merchandise not visible even to the buyer.' (The passage is from an
article collected in *The Knight's Move*, and is quoted by Victor Erlich in *Russian
Formalism*, New Haven 1955, p. 252.) This journey 'down the inevitable road
from birth to death' can however also be explained by focusing, not so much
on the relationship between the 'young' and the 'old' versions of the same form,
but rather on that between the form and its historical context: a genre exhausts
its potentialities—and the time comes to give a competitor a chance—when its
inner form is no longer capable of representing the most significant aspects of
contemporary reality. At which point, either the genre loses its form under the
impact of reality, thereby disintegrating, or it turns its back to reality in the name
of form, becoming a 'dull epigone' indeed. (I develop this point in the appendix
to the new edition of *The Way of the World*, '"A useless longing for myself": The
crisis of the European *Bildungsroman*, 1898–1914', London 2000.) But we will
soon see another, more draconian explanation for the disappearance of forms.

seem indeed to follow a rather regular 'life-cycle', as some econo-
mists would call it. These genres—or *all* genres? Is this wave-like
pattern a sort of hidden pendulum of literary history?

Here, the gathering of data is obviously crucial, and I decided to rely
entirely on other people's work: since we are all eager to find what we
are looking for, using the evidence gathered by other scholars, with
completely different research programmes, is always a good correc-
tive to one's desires. So, first Brad Pasanek, at Stanford, and then
I, consulted over a hundred studies of British genres between 1740
and 1900; there were some dubious cases, of course, and some (not
very significant) disagreements in periodization;[8] and although this
is still very much work-in-progress, especially at the two ends of the
temporal spectrum, the forty-four genres of figure 9 provide a large
enough set to support some reflections.

Forty-four genres over 160 years; but instead of finding one new genre
every four years or so, as a random distribution would have it, over
two thirds of them cluster in just thirty years, divided in six major
bursts of creativity: the late 1760s, early 1790s, late 1820s, 1850, early
1870s, and mid–late 1880s. And the genres also tend to *disappear* in
clusters: with the exception of the turbulence of 1790–1810, a rather
regular changing of the guard takes place, where half a dozen genres
quickly leave the scene, as many move in, and then remain in place
for twenty-five years or so. Instead of changing all the time and a
little at a time, then, the system stands still for decades, and is then
'punctuated' by brief bursts of invention: forms change once, rapidly,
across the board, and then repeat themselves for two–three decades:
'normal literature', we could call it, in analogy to Kuhn's normal

---

[8] When specialists disagreed, I always opted for the periodization arising out of
the more convincing morphological argument: in the case of industrial novels, for
instance, I followed Gallagher rather than Cazamian, although the latter's periodization of 1830–50 would have fitted my argument much better than Gallagher's
1832–67. For details, see 'A Note on the Taxonomy of the Forms', p. 31.

FIGURE 9: *British novelistic genres, 1740–1900*

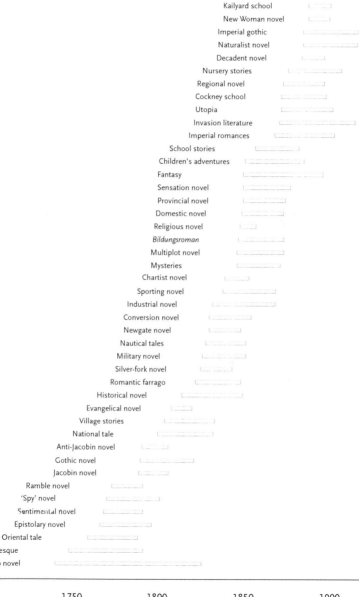

| | 1700 | 1750 | 1800 | 1850 | 1900 |

Kailyard school
New Woman novel
Imperial gothic
Naturalist novel
Decadent novel
Nursery stories
Regional novel
Cockney school
Utopia
Invasion literature
Imperial romances
School stories
Children's adventures
Fantasy
Sensation novel
Provincial novel
Domestic novel
Religious novel
Bildungsroman
Multiplot novel
Mysteries
Chartist novel
Sporting novel
Industrial novel
Conversion novel
Newgate novel
Nautical tales
Military novel
Silver-fork novel
Romantic farrago
Historical novel
Evangelical novel
Village stories
National tale
Anti-Jacobin novel
Gothic novel
Jacobin novel
Ramble novel
'Spy' novel
Sentimental novel
Epistolary novel
Oriental tale
Picaresque
Courtship novel

For sources, see 'A Note on the Taxonomy of the Forms', page 31.

science. Or think of Jauss's 'horizon of expectations': a metaphor we tend to evoke only 'negatively' (that is to say, when a text transcends the given horizon), but which these graphs present instead, 'positively', for what it is: figures 7–8 showing how difficult it actually is to transcend the hegemonic horizon, figure 9 presenting the multiple horizons active at any given moment, and so on.

VI

Normal literature remains in place for twenty-five years or so . . . But where does this rhythm come from? Shklovsky's hypothesis (however modified) cannot explain it, because the connexion between the decline of an old form and the rise of a new one implies nothing about the regularity of the replacement. And widespread regularity: not just the few hegemonic genres, but (almost) all genres active at any given time seem to arise and disappear together according to some hidden rhythm.

The simultaneity of the turnover, at first sight so uncanny, is probably the key to the solution. When one genre replaces another, it's reasonable to assume that the cause is internal to the two genres, and historically specific: amorous epistolary fiction being ill-equipped to capture the traumas of the revolutionary years, say—and gothic novels being particularly good at it. But when several genres disappear *together* from the literary field, and then another group, and so on, then the reason has to be different, because all these forms cannot have run *independently and simultaneously* into insoluble problems—it would be simply too much of a coincidence. The causal mechanism must thus be *external* to the genres, and *common* to all: like a sudden, total change of their ecosystem. Which is to say: a change of their audience. Books survive if they are read and disappear if they aren't: and when an entire generic system vanishes at once, the likeliest explanation is that *its readers vanished at once.*

This, then, is where those 25–30 years come from: generations. Not a concept I am very fond of, actually, but the only one that seems to make sense of figure 9. And indeed, in Mannheim's great essay of 1927, the best evidence for his thesis comes precisely from the aesthetic sphere: 'a rhythm in the sequence of generations', he writes, following Mentré's *Les générations sociales*, published a few years earlier,

> is far more apparent in the realm of the *séries libres*—free human groupings such as salons and literary circles—than in the realm of the institutions, which for the most part lay down a lasting pattern of behaviour, either by prescriptions or by the organization of collective undertakings, thus preventing the new generation from showing its originality . . . The aesthetic sphere is perhaps the most appropriate to reflect overall changes of mental climate.[9]

Overall changes of the mental climate: the five, six shifts in the British novelistic field between 1740 and 1900. But since people are born every day, not every twenty-five years, on what basis can the biological continuum be segmented into discrete units? Mannheim again:

> Whether a new *generation style* emerges every year, every thirty, every hundred years, or whether it emerges rhythmically at all, depends entirely on the trigger action of the social and cultural process . . . We shall therefore speak of a *generation as an actuality* only where a concrete bond is created between members of a generation by their being exposed to the social and intellectual symptoms of a process of dynamic destabilization.[10]

A bond due to a process of dynamic destabilization; and one who was eighteen in 1968 understands. But again, this cannot possibly explain the *regularity* of generational replacement, unless one assumes—absurdly—that the 'destabilizations' themselves occur punctually every twenty-five or thirty years. And so, I close on a note

[9] Karl Mannheim, 'The Problem of Generations', in *Essays on the Sociology of Knowledge*, London 1952, p. 279.
[10] *Essays on the Sociology of Knowledge*, pp. 303, 310.

of perplexity: *faute de mieux,* some kind of generational mechanism seems the best way to account for the regularity of the novelistic cycle—but 'generation' is itself a very questionable concept. Clearly, we must do better.[11]

VII

Normal literature remains in place for a generation or so . . . It's the central group of figure 10, which rearranges the forty-four genres according to their duration, and where about two thirds of them last indeed between 23 and 35 years.[12] The one large exception is formed by those genres—nine years, ten, twelve—on the left end of the spectrum: why so short-lived? Almost certainly, because of politics again: Jacobin, anti-Jacobin, evangelical novels around the turn of the century,

---

[11] A possible solution: at some point, a particularly significant 'destabilization' gives rise to a clearly defined generation, which occupies centre stage for 20–30 years, attracting within its orbit, and shaping after its mould, slightly younger or older individuals. Once biological age pushes this generation to the periphery of the cultural system, there is suddenly room for a new generation, which comes into being simply *because it can,* destabilization or not; and so on, and on. A regular series would thus emerge even without a 'trigger action' *for each new generation*: once the generational clock has been set in motion, it will run its course—for some time at least. (This is in fact Mentré's approach to the problem, especially in the long chapter in which he sketches an unbroken series of generations throughout French literature from 1515 to 1915.)
[12] A first look at French literature from the seventeenth to the nineteenth century suggests that most of its narrative genres have a similar 30-year span: pastoral and heroic novels, the *nouvelle historique, romans galants* and *contes philosophiques,* sentimental novels, the *Bildungsroman,* the *roman gai,* the two main phases ('heroic' and 'sentimental') of the *roman-feuilleton* . . . On the other hand, Sandra Guardini Vasconcelos and other Brazilian literary historians have pointed out that when a country *imports* most of its novels, the regular turnover of the Anglo-French generations is replaced by a much more accelerated and possibly uneven tempo. If they are right—and I think they are—then the Western European case would once more be the exception rather than the rule of world literature.

FIGURE 10: *British novelistic genres, 1740–1915 (duration in years)*

In this figure, the most striking exception are the eighty years of Katherine Sobba Green's periodization for 'courtship novels'. However, for most historians (and in part for Green herself) this genre goes through two quite distinct phases: the first from 1740 to 1780, dominated by the transcendent principle of chastity; and the second from 1780 (or, better, 1782, when Burney, in Cecilia, abandons the epistolary form) to 1820, dominated by the fundamentally immanent notion of manners. If one accepts this distinction, the anomaly disappears.

For sources, see 'A Note on the Taxonomy of the Forms', page 31.

Chartist and religious narratives in the 1840s, New Woman novels in the 1890s . . . And as often happens with politics and the novel, the outcome is a string of explicit ideological declarations: Jacobin novels trying to reform their villains by 'discussion and reasoning', as Gary Kelly puts it; Right Reason, adds Marilyn Butler in *Jane Austen and the War of Ideas*: a 'puzzling' choice, she goes on, the great 'missed opportunity' of the Jacobin novel as a form. Missed opportunity, yes, but puzzling, perhaps not: if a novel wants to engage the political sphere directly, a series of unambiguous statements, however narratively dull, is a perfectly rational choice. And then, ideological exchanges are an easy way to capture Braudel's 'dramatic rush of the event': to turn a book into *A tale of the times*, *A tale of the day*, *The philosophy of the day*, to quote some typical 1790s subtitles. But the conjunction of course works both ways: if what most attracts readers is the drama of the day, then, once the day is over, so is the novel . . .

VIII

Why did most British genres last 25–30 years, then, but some of them only ten? Because these 'political' forms subordinated narrative logic to the tempo of the short span, I have conjectured, and thus they also disappeared with the short span; and I hope the answer sounds plausible. But the real point, here, is less the specific answer, than the total *heterogeneity of problem and solution*: to make sense of quantitative data, I had to abandon the quantitative universe, and turn to morphology: evoke form, in order to explain figures. Here, the figures of the literary market. But when I studied the international impact of American films, I encountered exactly the same problematic: in the sample decade (1986–95), comedies amounted to 20% of the top box office hits within the United States, whereas elsewhere, as figure 11 shows, they were a lot less successful (especially in Asia and in the Mediterranean).[13] The figures were crystal clear. But if one then

---

[13] 'Planet Hollywood', New Left Review 9, May–June 2001, pp. 90–101.

FIGURE 11: *US comedies as a percentage of top five box office hits, 1986–95*

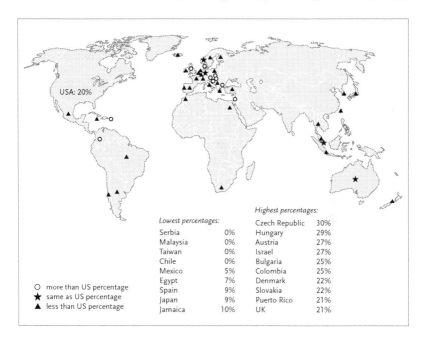

Lowest percentages:		Highest percentages:	
Serbia	0%	Czech Republic	30%
Malaysia	0%	Hungary	29%
Taiwan	0%	Austria	27%
Chile	0%	Israel	27%
Mexico	5%	Bulgaria	25%
Egypt	7%	Colombia	25%
Spain	9%	Denmark	22%
Japan	9%	Slovakia	22%
Jamaica	10%	Puerto Rico	21%
		UK	21%

O more than US percentage
★ same as US percentage
▲ less than US percentage

USA: 20%

wondered *why* this was so—why, in other words, comedies were so much harder to export than, say, action films—percentages offered no help, and the explanation had to be sought once again in the realm of form: as contemporary comedies make large use of jokes, which are often lost in translation, American comedies are quite simply a lot less funny in Japanese or Egyptian or Spanish than in English. (Not for nothing, the great international age of comic films—Chaplin, Keaton, Lloyd, Laurel and Hardy—coincided with silent cincma.)[14]

[14] See here how a quantitative history of literature is also a profoundly formalist one—especially at the beginning and at the end of the research process. At the end, for the reasons we have just seen; and at the beginning, because a formal concept is usually what makes quantification possible in the first place: since a series must be composed of homogeneous objects, a morphological category is needed—'novel', 'anti-Jacobin novel', 'comedy', etc—to establish such homogeneity.

Quantification poses the problem, then, and form offers the solution. But let me add: if you are lucky. Because the asymmetry of a quantitative *explanandum* and a qualitative *explanans* leaves you often with a perfectly clear problem—and no idea of a solution. In 'Planet Hollywood', for instance, it turned out that absolutely *all* Italian box office hits of the sample decade were comedies; why that was so, however, was completely unclear. I felt I had to say something, so I presented an 'explanation', and NLR indulgently printed it; but it was silly of me, because the most interesting aspect of those data was that *I had found a problem for which I had absolutely no solution.* And problems without a solution are exactly what we need in a field like ours, where we are used to asking only those questions for which we already have an answer. 'I have noticed,' says Brecht's Herr Keuner, 'that we put many people off our teaching because we have an answer to everything. Could we not, in the interest of propaganda, draw up a list of the questions that appear to us completely unsolved?'

IX

Two brief theoretical conclusions. The first is again on the cycle as the hidden thread of literary history. 'For the elevation of the novel to occur', writes William Warner in *Licensing Entertainment*, 'the novel of amorous intrigue must . . . disappear'; it is 'the Great Gender Shift' of the mid-eighteenth century, adds April Alliston: the disappearance of earlier fiction by women writers, with the related increase in the number of male novelists. And it's all true, except for the article: *the* shift? The third quarter of the nineteenth century, write Tuchman and Fortin in *Edging Women Out*, was 'the period of invasion' of the novelistic field by male authors, who eventually 'edge out' their female competitors.[15]

---

[15] William B. Warner, *Licensing Entertainment. The Elevation of Novel Reading in Britain, 1685–1750*, Berkeley 1998, p. 44; April Alliston, 'Love in Excess', in *Il romanzo*, vol. 1, *La cultura del romanzo*, Torino 2001, p. 650; Gaye Tuchman and Nina Fortin, *Edging Women Out*, New Haven 1989, pp. 7–8.

But, clearly, a mid-Victorian 'invasion' presupposes a reversal of the gender shift of the 1740s. And, in fact, this is what the historical record shows: if between 1750 and 1780, as a result of the initial shift, men publish indeed twice as many novels as women, in the late 1780s a second shift reverses the gender ratio, as one can see in Garside's breakdown for a slightly later period (figure 12, overleaf), in which women novelists (among them Burney, Radcliffe, Edgeworth, Austen) remain the majority until a third shift occurs, around 1820, towards male writers (Scott; then Bulwer, Dickens, Thackeray), to be followed by a fourth shift back to women in mid-century (the Brontës, Gaskell, Braddon, Eliot), and then by a fifth one—the 'edging out'— in the 1870s. Similar data are beginning to emerge for France, Spain, the US, and it's fascinating to see how researchers are convinced that they are all describing something unique (*the* gender shift, *the* elevation of the novel, *the* gentrification, *the* invention of high and low, *the* feminization, *the* sentimental education, *the* invasion . . .), whereas in all likelihood they are all observing the same comet that keeps crossing and recrossing the sky: the same *literary cycle*, where gender and genre are probably in synchrony with each other—a generation of military novels, nautical tales, and historical novels *à la* Scott attracting male writers, one of domestic, provincial and sensation novels attracting women writers, and so on.

Now, let me be clear, saying that these studies describe the return of the same literary cycle is not an objection: quite the opposite, my thesis *depends* on their findings, and it even corroborates them somehow, by finding the common mechanism which is at work in all those instances. But it's also true that if one reframes individual instances as moments of a cycle, then the nature of the questions changes: 'Events don't interest Lucien Febvre for what in them is unique', writes Pomian, but 'as units in a series, which reveal the conjunctural variations in . . . a conflict that remains constant throughout the period.'[16]

[16] Pomian, 'L'histoire des structures', p. 117.

FIGURE 12: *Authorship of new novels, Britain 1800–1829: gender breakdown (percentage)*

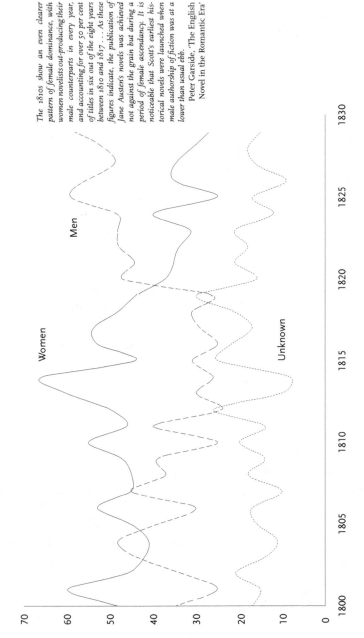

The 1810s show an even clearer pattern of female dominance, with women novelists out-producing their male counterparts in every year, and accounting for over 50 per cent of titles in six out of the eight years between 1810 and 1817 . . . As these figures indicate, the publication of Jane Austen's novels was achieved not against the grain but during a period of female ascendancy. It is noticeable that Scott's earliest historical novels were launched when male authorship of fiction was at a lower than usual ebb.

Peter Garside, 'The English Novel in the Romantic Era'

Source: Garside, Raven and Schöwerling, eds, *The English Novel 1770–1829.*

Variations in a conflict that remains constant: this is what emerges at the level of the cycle—and if the conflict remains constant, then the point is not who prevails in this or that skirmish, but exactly the opposite: no victory is ever definitive, neither men nor women writers 'occupy' the British novel once and for all, and the form keeps oscillating back and forth between the two groups. And if this sounds like nothing is happening, no, what is happening *is the oscillation*, which allows the novel to use a double pool of talents and of forms, thereby boosting its productivity, and giving it an edge over its many competitors. But this process can only be glimpsed *at the level of the cycle*: individual episodes tend, if anything, to conceal it, and only the abstract pattern reveals the true nature of the historical process.[17]

X

Do cycles and genres explain everything, in the history of the novel? Of course not. But they bring to light its hidden tempo, and suggest some questions on what we could call its internal shape. For most literary historians, I mean, there is a categorical difference between 'the novel' and the various 'novelistic (sub)genres': the novel is, so to speak, the substance of the form, and deserves a full general

---

[17] A comparable oscillation is probably at work between High and Low forms, whose simultaneous existence is a well-known, if often ignored, fact of novelistic history: from the Hellenistic beginnings (divided between 'subliterary' and 'idealized' genres) through the Middle Ages, the seventeenth century (the *Bibliothèque Bleue*, and aristocratic novels), eighteenth (Warner's pair of 'entertainment' and 'elevation'), nineteenth (*feuilletons*, railway novels—and 'serious realism'), and twentieth century (pulp fiction—modernist experiments). Here, too, the strength of the novel is not to be found in *one* of the two positions, but in its rhythmical oscillation between them: the novel is not hegemonic because it makes it into High Culture (it does, yes, but it's so desperately professorial to be awed by this fact), but for the opposite reason: it is never *only* in High Culture, and it can keep playing on two tables, preserving its double nature, where vulgar and refined are almost inextricable.

theory; subgenres are more like accidents, and their study, however interesting, remains local in character, without real theoretical consequences. The forty-four genres of figure 9, however, suggest a different historical picture, where the novel does not develop as a single entity—where is 'the' novel, there?—but by periodically generating a whole set of genres, and then another, and another . . . Both synchronically and diachronically, in other words, the novel is *the system of its genres*: the whole diagram, not one privileged part of it. Some genres are morphologically more significant, of course, or more popular, or both—and we must account for this: but not by pretending that they are the only ones that exist. And instead, all great theories of the novel have precisely reduced the novel to one basic form only (realism, the dialogic, romance, meta-novels . . .); and if the reduction has given them their elegance and power, it has also erased nine tenths of literary history. Too much.

I began this chapter by saying that quantitative data are useful because they are independent of interpretation; then, that they are challenging because they often demand an interpretation that transcends the quantitative realm; now, most radically, we see them *falsify* existing theoretical explanations, and ask for a theory, not so much of 'the' novel, but of *a whole family of novelistic forms*. A theory—of diversity. What this may mean, will be the topic of my third chapter.

A NOTE ON THE TAXONOMY OF THE FORMS

The genres of figures 9 and 10 are listed below in the following way: current definition (in capitals); dates of beginning and end; and critical study from which I have drawn the chosen (and not always explicit) periodization. Since both figures are meant as a first panorama of a very large territory, soon to be improved by further work, a few words of caution are in order. First, except for the (rare) cases in which quantitative data or full bibliographies are available, the initial date refers to the genre's first recognizable example rather than to its genuine take-off, which occurs usually several years later; as our knowledge improves, therefore, it is likely that the chronological span of novelistic genres will turn out to be significantly shorter than the one given here. On the other hand, a few genres experience brief but intense revivals decades after their original peak, like the oriental tale in 1819–25, or the gothic after 1885, or the historical novel (more than once). How to account for these Draculaesque reawakenings is a fascinating topic, which however will have to wait for another occasion. Finally, the chart shows neither detective fiction nor science fiction; although both genres achieve their modern form around 1890 (Doyle and Wells), and undergo a major change in the 1920s, in step with the overall pattern, their peculiar long duration seems to require a different approach.

COURTSHIP NOVEL, 1740–1820: Katherine Sobba Green, *The Courtship Novel 1740–1820*, Kentucky 1991. PICARESQUE, 1748–90: F. W. Chandler, *The Literature of Roguery*, London 1907. ORIENTAL TALE, 1759–87: Ernest Baker, *The History of the English Novel*, London 1924, vol. v. EPISTOLARY NOVEL, 1766–95: James Raven, 'Historical Introduction', in Garside, Raven and Schöwerling, eds, *The English Novel 1770–1829*, vol. I. SENTIMENTAL NOVEL, 1768–90: John Mullan,

'Sentimental Novels', in John Richetti, ed., *The Cambridge Companion to the Eighteenth-Century Novel*, Cambridge 1996. 'SPY' NOVEL, 1770–1800: Christopher Flint, 'Speaking Objects: The Circulation of Stories in Eighteenth-Century Prose Fiction', PMLA 113 (2), March 1998, pp. 212–26. RAMBLE NOVEL, 1773–90: Simon Dickie, *The Mid-Century 'Ramble' Novels*, PhD dissertation, Stanford 2000. JACOBIN NOVEL, 1789–1805: Gary Kelly, *The English Jacobin Novel 1780–1805*, Oxford 1976. GOTHIC NOVEL, 1790–1820: Peter Garside, 'The English Novel in the Romantic Era', in Garside, Raven and Schöwerling, eds, *The English Novel 1770–1829*, vol. II. ANTI-JACOBIN NOVEL, 1791–1805: M. O. Grenby, *The Anti-Jacobin Novel*, Cambridge 2001. NATIONAL TALE, 1800–31: Katie Trumpener, 'National Tale', in Paul Schellinger, ed., *The Encyclopedia of the Novel*, Chicago 1998, vol. II. VILLAGE STORIES, 1804–32: Gary Kelly, *English Fiction of the Romantic Period, 1789–1830*, London 1989. EVANGELICAL NOVEL, 1808–19: Peter Garside, 'The English Novel in the Romantic Era'. HISTORICAL NOVEL, 1814–48: Nicholas Rance, *The Historical Novel and Popular Politics in Nineteenth-Century England*, New York 1975. ROMANTIC FARRAGO, 1822–47: Gary Kelly, *English Fiction of the Romantic Period*. SILVER-FORK NOVEL, 1825–42: Alison Adburgham, *Silver Fork Society*, London 1983. MILITARY NOVEL, 1826–50: Peter Garside, 'The English Novel in the Romantic Era'. NAUTICAL TALES, 1828–50: Michael Wheeler, *English Fiction of the Victorian Period: 1830–90*, London 1985. NEWGATE NOVEL, 1830–47: Keith Hollingsworth, *The Newgate Novel, 1830–47*, Detroit 1963. CONVERSION NOVEL, 1830–53: Sarah Gracombe, *Anxieties of Influence: Jewishness and English Culture in the Victorian Novel*, PhD dissertation, Columbia University 2003. INDUSTRIAL NOVEL, 1832–67: Catherine Gallagher, *The Industrial Reformation of English Fiction*, Chicago 1985. SPORTING NOVEL, 1838–67: John Sutherland, *The Stanford Companion to Victorian Literature*, Stanford 1989. CHARTIST NOVEL, 1839–52: Gustav Klaus, *The Literature of Labour*, New York 1985. MYSTERIES, 1846–70: Richard Maxwell, *The Mysteries of Paris and London*, Charlottesville, VA 1992. MULTIPLOT NOVEL, 1846–72: Crisi Benford, *The Multiplot Novel and*

Victorian Culture, PhD dissertation, Stanford 2003. BILDUNGSROMAN, 1847–72: Michael Minden, 'Bildungsroman', in Schellinger, ed., *The Encyclopedia of the Novel*, vol. II. RELIGIOUS NOVEL, 1848–56: Wheeler, *English Fiction of the Victorian Period*. DOMESTIC NOVEL, 1849–72: Sutherland, *Stanford Companion to Victorian Literature*. PROVINCIAL NOVEL, 1850–73: Ian Duncan, 'The Provincial or Regional Novel', in Patrick Brantlinger and William Thesing, eds, *A Companion to the Victorian Novel*, Oxford 2003. SENSATION NOVEL, 1850–76: Nicholas Rance, *Wilkie Collins and Other Sensation Novelists*, London 1991. FANTASY, 1850–95: C. N. Manlove, *Modern Fantasy: Five Studies*, Cambridge 1975. CHILDREN'S ADVENTURES, 1851–83: Sutherland, *Stanford Companion to Victorian Literature*. SCHOOL STORIES, 1857–81: Isabel Quigly, *The Heirs of Tom Brown*, London 1982. IMPERIAL ROMANCES, 1868–1902: Joseph Bristow, *Empire Boys*, London 1991. INVASION LITERATURE, 1871–14: I. F. Clarke, *The Tale of the Next Great War, 1871–1914*, Liverpool 1995. UTOPIA, 1872–1901: Wheeler, *English Fiction of the Victorian Period*. COCKNEY SCHOOL, 1872–97: Sutherland, *Stanford Companion to Victorian Literature*. REGIONAL NOVEL, 1873–96: Duncan, 'The Provincial or Regional Novel'. NURSERY STORIES, 1876–1906: Gillian Avery, *Nineteenth Century Children*, London 1965. DECADENT NOVEL, 1884–1906: A. A. Mandal, 'Decadent Novel', in Schellinger, ed., *The Encyclopedia of the Novel*, vol. I. NATURALIST NOVEL, 1885–1915: William Frierson, *L'influence du naturalisme français sur les romanciers anglais de 1885 à 1900*, Paris 1925. IMPERIAL GOTHIC, 1885–1916: Patrick Brantlinger, *Rule of Darkness*, Ithaca 1988. NEW WOMAN NOVEL, 1888–99: Ann L. Ardis, *New Women, New Novels*, New Brunswick 1990. KAILYARD SCHOOL, 1888–1900: Sutherland, *Stanford Companion to Victorian Literature*.

Maps

There is a very simple question about literary maps: what exactly do they *do*? What do they do that cannot be done with words, that is; because, if it can be done with words, then maps are superfluous. Take Bakhtin's essay on the chronotope: it is the greatest study ever written on space and narrative, and it doesn't have a single map. Carlo Dionisotti's *Geografia e storia della letteratura italiana*, the same. Raymond Williams's *The Country and the City*, the same. Henri Lafon's *Espaces romanesques du XVIIIe siècle* . . . Do maps *add* anything, to our knowledge of literature?

I

Village stories were a popular British genre of the first quarter of the nineteenth century, peaking with Mary Mitford's *Our Village*, published in five volumes between 1824 and 1832. The village was Three Mile Cross, in Berkshire (figure 13, overleaf), a dozen miles south of Reading, on the road to Hampshire; and the road is explicitly foregrounded in Mitford's opening sketch, where it also forms the basis for her presentation of the village as one house after another along a 'straggling, winding street'. So you think, 'Yonville',[1] and imagine

[1] 'There is nothing further to see in Yonville. The street, the only one, about a gunshot in length, with a few shops on each side . . .' (*Madame Bovary*, II.1)

FIGURE 13: *Three Mile Cross*

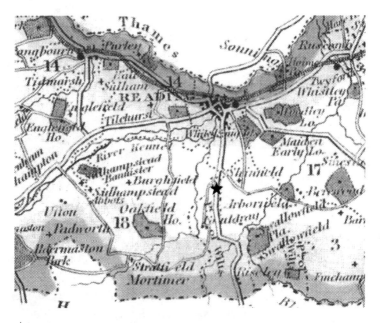

★   Three Mile Cross

A small neighbourhood is as good in sober waking reality as in poetry or prose; a village neighbour-hood, such as this Berkshire hamlet in which I write, a long, straggling, winding street, at the bottom of a fine eminence, with a road through it, always abounding in carts, horsemen and carriages, and lately enlivened by a stage-coach from B– to S–.

Mary Mitford, 'Our Village'

Source: Thomas Moule, *The English Counties Delineated* [1837], London 1994

this village of two or three hundred people as a mere site of tran-sit between larger places (*Effi Briest*: 'no, the Gdansk–Berlin express does not stop here . . .'). Easy.

Then you make a map of the book, and everything changes. The twenty-four stories of Mitford's first volume, figure 14 shows, arrange themselves in a little solar system, with the village at the centre of the

FIGURE 14: *Mary Mitford,* Our Village, *volume 1 [1824]*

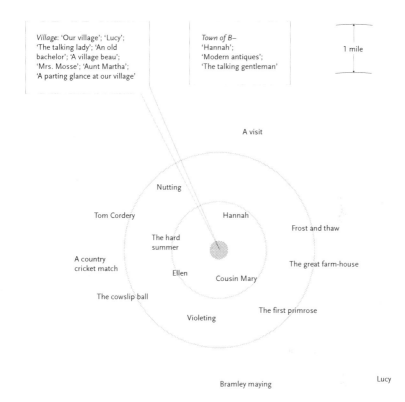

pattern, and two roughly concentric rings around it. The first ring is closer to the village, and focuses largely on personal relationships ('Ellen', 'Hannah', 'Cousin Mary'); the second ring, its components more numerous, is at a distance of a couple of miles, and emphasizes natural spectacles ('Frost and thaw', 'Violeting', 'The first primrose'), plus collective events like cricket and maying. But in both cases the road 'from B– to S–', so present at the beginning of the book, has disappeared: narrative space is not linear here, it is *circular*. Which is surprising: while mapping nineteenth-century genres for the *Atlas of the European Novel* I encountered all sorts of shapes—linear trajectories, binary fields, triangulations, multi-polar stories—but never a circular pattern. Where on earth do these rings come from?

II

John Barrell, *The Idea of Landscape and the Sense of Place 1730–1840*:

> There is a sense in which an open-field parish in the late eighteenth and early nineteenth centuries [which is exactly what the one in *Our Village* is like] could be said to have a different geography according to who was looking at it: thus, for those of its inhabitants who rarely went beyond the parish boundary, the parish itself was so to speak at the centre of the landscape . . . For those inhabitants accustomed to moving outside it, however, and for those travellers who passed through it, the parish was . . . defined not by some circular system of geography but by a linear one.[2]

A circular 'system of geography', and a linear one: behind these two perspectives lies the dramatic transformation of rural space produced by parliamentary enclosure, which Barrell has so well visualized in his two maps of Helpston, and where a perceptual (because productive) system in which the village is still largely self-sufficient, and can therefore feel at the centre of 'its own' space, is replaced by an abstract grid, within which Helpston becomes just one of the many 'beads' that the various roads will run through (figures 15–16, overleaf).

Against this background, *Our Village*'s spatial pattern becomes at once clearer, and more surprising: by opening with a linear perspective, and then shifting to a circular one, Mitford reverses the direction

---

[2] John Barrell, *The Idea of Landscape and the Sense of Place 1730–1840*, Cambridge 1972, p. 95. For the sources of the two Helpston maps (figures 15–16), see pp. 225–7.

of history, making her urban readers (*Our Village* was published by Whitaker, Ave-Maria-Lane, London) look at the world according to the older, 'centred' viewpoint of an unenclosed village. And the key to this perceptual shift lies in Mitford's most typical episode: the country walk. In story after story, the young narrator leaves the village, each time in a different direction, reaches the destinations charted in figure 14, then turns around and goes home. 'When a system is free to spread its energy in space', writes Rudolf Arnheim, 'it sends out its vectors evenly all around, like the rays emanating from a source of light. The resulting . . . pattern is the prototype of *centric composition*.'[3] Exactly: out of the free movements of *Our Village*'s narrator, spread evenly all around like the petals of a daisy, a circular pattern crystallizes—as it does, we shall see, in *all* village stories, of which it constitutes the fundamental chronotope. But in order to see this pattern, we must first extract it from the narrative flow, and the only way to do so is with a map. Not, of course, that the map is already an explanation; but at least it shows us that there is something *that needs to be explained*. One step at a time.

III

A rounded pattern in Helpston before the enclosure; and a rounded pattern in *Our Village*. But with a difference: in Mitford's walks, Barrell's 'rough circle . . . in which the villagers work and move' is rewritten as a space of *leisure* rather than work. Slow easy strolls, thoughtless, happy, in the company of a greyhound called May; all around, a countryside full of picturesque natural views, but where very few people are actually doing anything. Decorative: for each page devoted to agricultural labour, there must be twenty on flowers and trees, described with meticulous precision. If urban readers are

---

[3] Rudolf Arnheim, *The Power of the Center. A Study of Composition in the Visual Arts*, new version, Berkeley and Los Angeles 1988, p. 4.

FIGURE 15: *The parish of Helpston in 1809, before the enclosure*

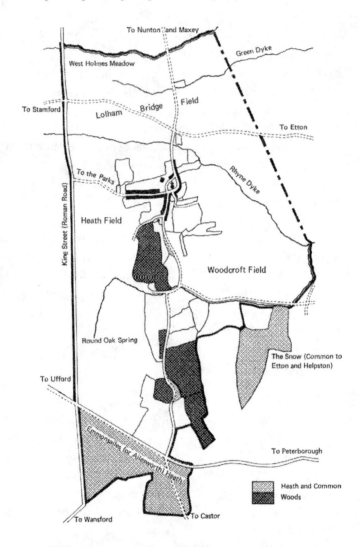

To Nunton and Maxey

Green Dyke

West Holmes Meadow

To Stamford

Lolham Bridge Field

To Etton

King Street (Roman Road)

To the Parks

Rhyne Dyke

Heath Field

Woodcroft Field

Round Oak Spring

The Snow (Common to
Etton and Helpston)

To Ufford

Commons (or Ailsworth) Heath

To Peterborough

Heath and Common

Woods

To Wansford

To Castor

The characteristic sense of space which the topography and organization of an open-field parish created was circular, while the landscape of parliamentary enclosure expressed a more linear sense . . . the village of Helpston is at the centre of the parish, where the three fields of the parish come together: they form around the settlement a rough circle, which represents the area in which the villagers work and move.

John Barrell, *The Idea of Landscape and the Sense of Place 1730–1840*

FIGURE 16: *The parish of Helpston in 1820, after the enclosure*

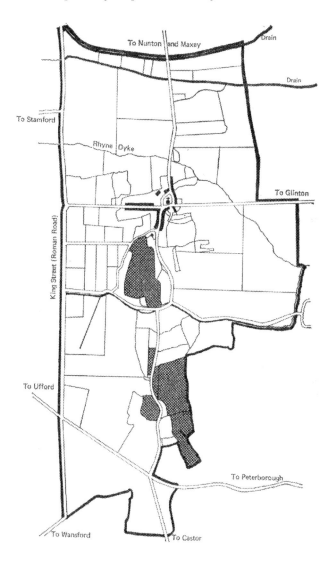

To Nunton and Maxey | Drain

Drain

To Stamford

Rhyne Dyke

To Glinton

King Street (Roman Road)

To Ufford

To Peterborough

To Wansford | To Castor

Priest's idea of a road is that it should be threaded through one village and another like a string through beads: he thinks of the road as in some sense prior to the villages on it, and not of the villages existing separately first.

John Barrell, *The Idea of Landscape and the Sense of Place 1730–1840*

made to share the village's perception of space, then, it's also true that this space has been thoroughly *gentrified*; as if Mitford had travelled forward in time, and discovered what city-dwellers will want to find in the countryside during a brief weekend visit. Not surprisingly, country walks were by far the most popular part of *Our Village*, and remained long in print by themselves while the rest was forgotten.

Behind the similarity of figures 14 and 15, then, lie very different experiences of social space. Barrell's 1809 'system of geography' corresponds to the omnipresent, half-submerged culture of daily routines—position of the fields, local paths, perception of distances, horizon—which historians tend to call *mentalité*, and which is often entwined with the performance of material labour. Mitford's neat stylization of rural space, however—with its alchemical transmutation of the 'rough circle' of work into a ring of pleasure—is not *mentalité*, but rather *ideology*: the world-view of a different social actor (an urban visitor), whose movements duplicate the perimeter of rural *mentalité*, but completely reverse its symbolic associations.

A map of ideology emerging from a map of *mentalité*, emerging from the material substratum of the physical territory. Granted, things are not always so neat. But when they are, it's interesting.

IV

The formula just used for Mitford—a 'stylization' of space—is even more appropriate for Walter Christaller's classic study on *Central Places in Southern Germany*. Written in the early Thirties, the book explains the geographical distribution of urban centres on the basis of the 'ordering principle, heretofore unrecognized' of the spatial division of labour: towns provide specialized services, writes Christaller ('banking, administration, cultural and spiritual offerings [church, school, theatre, professional and business organizations], sanitation'), which in order to reach as many customers as possible are located in 'a few necessarily central points, to be consumed at many scattered points'.[4] The more specialized a service is, the more 'central' it also is, and on this socio-geometrical principle arises the urban hierarchy synthesized by Christaller himself in figure 17. The rule here is simple: around each G-centre of the first rank there is a 'market region' which includes six B-centres of the second rank, with

FIGURE 17: *Central Places*

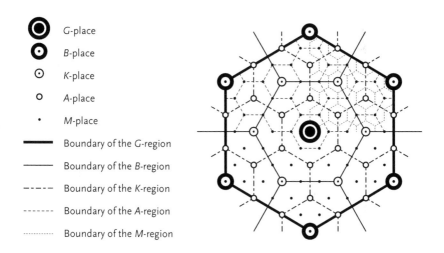

G-place

B-place

K-place

A-place

M-place

Boundary of the G-region

Boundary of the B-region

Boundary of the K-region

Boundary of the A-region

Boundary of the M-region

Source: *Central Places in Southern Germany*

[4] Walter Christaller, *Central Places in Southern Germany* [1933], Englewood Cliffs, NJ 1966, p. 20. Christaller's model presupposes an 'isotropic' space, where movement can occur with equal ease in every direction; this is of course a theoretical abstraction, whose empirical validity is limited to homogeneous agricultural flatlands (like indeed much of Southern Germany). The assumption of an isotropic space is the common denominator between Christaller's theory and the structure of village narratives; I briefly discuss the problematic nature of this idea in footnote 12 below.

fewer and less specialized services; around each B-centre there are six K-centres of the third rank, and so on, until, at the very bottom of the hierarchy, we encounter . . . *Our Village*: the 'central region of the lowest order', as Christaller calls it, whose radius (2–3 kilometres) is exactly the same as one of the book's country walks. And figure 18, Christaller-like, visualizes the services offered by Mitford's village, and by the other urban centres mentioned in her book.

In the village: shoemaker, blacksmith, carpenter, mason; in London and the other towns: French teachers, hatters, fashionable tailors, horse races. Serious daily needs versus frivolous superfluities: this is Mitford's social geography. Its roots are in one of the most ancient, and most widespread, of narrative forms: the idyll. 'Birth, labour, love, marriage, death', wrote Bakhtin of this *longue durée* chronotope: 'only a few of life's basic realities . . . a little world . . . sufficient unto itself, not linked in any intrinsic way with other places.'[5] Sufficient unto itself: this is why village stories organize themselves in circular patterns: a circle is a simple, 'natural' form, which maximizes the proximity of each point to the centre of the 'little world', while simultaneously sealing it off from the vast universe that lies outside its perimeter. 'Sugar and coffee and salt: we wanted nothing else from the outside world', declares proudly the protagonist of a German village story of the same period, Auerbach's *Brigitta*. But the past tense of that 'wanted' is a sign that the days of the idyll are numbered.

V

The changing geography of village narratives is particularly clear in another book of the 1820s, John Galt's *Annals of the Parish* (1821). The parish is Dalmailing, near the west coast of Scotland, and the

[5] Mikhail Bakhtin, 'Forms of Time and of the Chronotope in the Novel', 1937–38, in *The Dialogic Imagination*, Austin 1981, p. 225.

FIGURE 18: *Mary Mitford,* Our Village: *spatial division of labour*

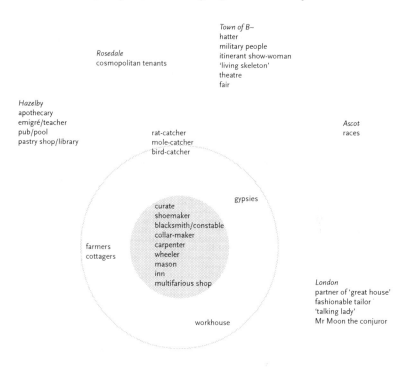

Town of B–
hatter
military people
itinerant show-woman
'living skeleton'
theatre
fair

Rosedale
cosmopolitan tenants

Hazelby
apothecary
emigré/teacher
pub/pool
pastry shop/library

Ascot
races

rat-catcher
mole-catcher
bird-catcher

gypsies

curate
shoemaker
blacksmith/constable
collar-maker
carpenter
wheeler
mason
inn
multifarious shop

farmers
cottagers

London
partner of 'great house'
fashionable tailor
'talking lady'
Mr Moon the conjuror

workhouse

2 miles

There are two main methods by which one can distribute goods to the consumer: one can offer them at the central place to which the consumer must come, or one can travel with the goods and offer them to the consumer at his residence. The former method leads necessarily to the formation of central places or market places; the latter method, however, does not require central places. In earlier times, the travelling salesman was far more prevalent than he is today. The pedlar, the knife-sharpener, the wandering minstrel of the Middle Ages, and the travelling priest all brought goods to the consumer.
Walter Christaller, *Central Places in Southern Germany*

In *Our Village*, the curate, shoemaker, or inn are centripetal services, whereas rat-, mole- and bird-catcher—who are encountered outside of the village, and whose occupation lies, practically and symbolically, on the border between the human and the natural world—are instances of the older type, like the memorable 'reddleman' of *The Return of the Native*. The village's weak division of labour produces also many all-purpose entities like the 'multifarious bazaar' of the village shop, the blacksmith who doubles as a constable, or characters such as John Wilson, 'a handy fellow, who could do any sort of work—thatcher, carpenter, bricklayer, painter, gardener, gamekeeper . . .'

text covers the half century from 1760 to 1810: each year a chapter, where the minister Balwhidder registers the main events in the crowded and often confusing mode of annalistic writing (fires, weddings, wars, births, portents . . .), of which the first ten years of the book—charted in figure 19—offer a typical instance. Here, from the still idyllic daily life of Dalmailing, in the bottom left corner ('birth, labour, marriage, death . . .'), we can follow two possible threads through the figure's materials. The first runs through Irville (Irvine), Glasgow, and Edinburgh, and shows the system of central places at work: school in Irville, university in Glasgow, lawyers and doctors in Edinburgh; second-hand news in Irville, and first-hand news in Glasgow; celebration dinner, honeymoon, marble headstone . . . As services become more unusual, they move 'up' in the urban hierarchy, and further away from Dalmailing; but since Galt's world is still fundamentally one of simple everyday needs, such services are seldom required, and central places like Edinburgh or London remain barely visible.

Extremely visible on the other hand are the many 'novelties' listed in the second column from the left, which reach the parish from the West Indies, the Baltic, and other unspecified places. Behind them is the British empire, of course, but perhaps even more the sheer fact of *distance*: in Dalmailing, a parrot, Rososolus, or a *cocker-nut* (Balwhidder's half-Dutch spelling for coconut) are truly things from another world. Wonders. Or, more prosaically, luxuries; products of long-distance trade which shine for a moment on the horizon of the everyday, leaving behind a sense of incommensurable universes: on the one side birth, labour, marriage, and death; on the other, coconut, Riga balsam, parrot, and Danzig cordial. Home, and the World. But since the world does not really change everyday existence (its wonders are all singular: one donkey, one coconut, one bottle of this and that), the antithesis is at once radical, and totally irrelevant: wonders appear, are admired, and then vanish (except for tea, of course). The world is an astonishing place, but

FIGURE 19: John Galt, Annals of the Parish: first decade [1760–69]

America: rumours of rebellion

Norway: expansion of coal trade

Ireland 'wild Irish seeking work'

Dalmailing. Daily life
- arrival of pastor
- arrival of Mrs Malcolm
- marriages
- illegitimate children born
- twins born
- twin calves born
- smallpox
- 'natural wonder' [a toad]
- pastor's patron dies
- old schoolmaster dies
- pastor's wife dies
- distillator of herbs dies
- schoolmistress dies
- burning of the mill
- fire on local estate
- school closes/reopens
- smuggling
- haberdasher's shop opens
- king's road mended

Dalmailing. Novelties
- tea
- pear tree
- parrot
- coconut
- donkey
- mantua-making
- new names for children
- Riga balsam
- Rossolus
- Dantzick cordial
- first Dalmailing sailor
- alehouse

Irville [2–3 miles]:
- children to school
- news [second-hand]
- butter to market [regularly]
- inn provides celebration dinner
- inn provides chaise
- dancing master
- Belfast coal-bark

Various villages [5–10 miles radius]
- finds first wife
- finds second wife
- smuggling
- seamen
- shipmaster lost at sea
- coalpits sink

Glasgow [25 miles]:
- goes to university
- brother-in-law goes to college
- news [first hand]
- cheese to market [occasionally]
- new schoolmistress
- honeymoon
- many useful things
- mantua-making

Edinburgh [60 miles]:
- medical consultation
- old pupil becomes advocate
- marble headstone

gypsies

London
Lord Eglesham visits his lands

France
- prisoner returns
- man returns from war academy
- 'contrivances of French millinery'

India: a nabob

the Dalmailing idyll goes on as it always has, 'not linked in any intrinsic way to other places'.

But in 1788 a cotton-mill is built—'nothing like it had been seen before in our day and generation'—and with it the manufacturing town of Cayenneville, and the parish's spatial coordinates are forever changed. If one compares the first decade of the book with the last, charted in figure 20, it's impossible to miss the dramatic *re-centring* of social life induced by manufacture: the sense of the 'region', so strong a generation earlier—Dalmailing's daily life, the Irville where children went to school, the villages where spouses came from . . .—is gone, replaced by a 'web of commercial reciprocities' (Cayenneville–Glasgow–Manchester–London), whose 'every touch

FIGURE 20: *John Galt,* Annals of the Parish: *last decade [1801–10]*

Glasgow:
Catholic church opens
cotton mill manager goes to
company buys mill

Cayenneville [2–3 miles]:
a turtle
bookshop
London dailies
Jacobinism
Catholic church opens/closes
workers pay for their own church
company stops payment
overseer commits suicide

Manchester:
cotton mill overseer

'English engineer'

London:
concern owns share of Cayenneville
cotton mill manager goes to
overseer's orphan sent to

Dalmailing:
parish poet
inn buys its own chaise
village parade
relaxation of religious discipline
empty seats in church
new habits at funerals
marriages

France
fears of invasion

Year 1801: It is often to me very curious food for meditation, that as the parish increased in popula-tion, there should have been less cause for matter to record. Things that in former days would have occasioned great discourse and cogitation, are forgotten, with the day in which they happen . . .
John Galt, The Annals of the Parish

or stir [is] felt in our corner' (year 1808). Between Home and the World, a new spatial reality has wedged itself, subordinating them both: the national market, whose intermediate distance is traversed every week, if not day, by those *regular novelties*—books, newspapers, politics: all plurals—which will keep multiplying throughout the industrial nineteenth century. From the old Age of Wonders, only a turtle survives.

VI

One last collection, German this time. Berthold Auerbach's *Black Forest Village Stories*, written between 1843 and 1853, were among the great bestsellers of the century, and figure 21 (overleaf) charts about one third of the *Dorfgeschichten* collected in Cotta's 1940 ten-volume edition. Here, too, three spaces interact and compete for attention. The first is composed by Nordstetten and the other Black Forest villages, and its features should by now be familiar: narrow geographic range, daily needs, basic services—all contained within the same circular pattern we have encountered in Britain. But if the spatial logic of the idyll is more or less the same everywhere (probably because of its extreme narrative simplicity), Auerbach's international space is already quite different from Mitford's or Galt's: instead of sporadic wonders, we find war memories (Germany as 'the battlefield of Europe', in Thomas Mann's words), threats of economic competition, and especially the *basso continuo* of emigration (America, first of all; then Switzerland, France, Greece, Russia, Spain . . .). Except for Switzerland, which is very close, the narrative never actually moves into these foreign countries, but the voices of those who have left echo in almost every story, as if they were a large, hidden chorus. Nostalgic, usually; but in the more optimistic moments— like the letter from 'Nordstetten on the Ohio' ('we'll send for a parson from Germany. And my fields have just the same names

FIGURE 21: *Berthold Auerbach*, Black Forest Village Stories *[1843–53]*

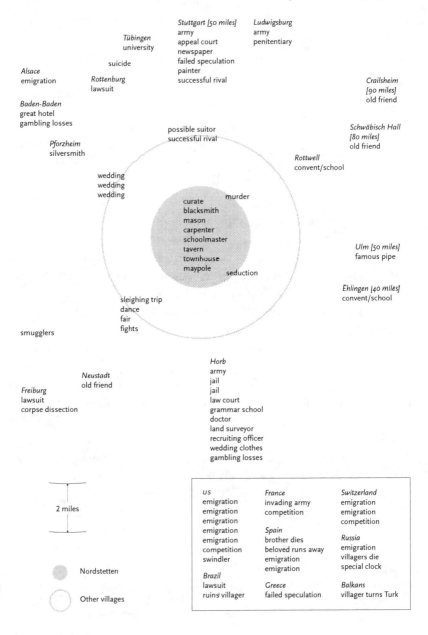

they used to have . . .')—also capable of looking at a distant land as almost a second home.

But in the meantime, just as earlier in Galt, a third, quasi-national space ('quasi', because German unity is still a generation away), is forcing its way into village life through 'central places' such as Horb, Freiburg, Rottenburg and Stuttgart. What we find there, though, is not manufacture, banks, and services, as in Britain, but law courts, jails, army barracks, and the like. The state. The state *as repression*: a grim determination to achieve the monopoly of legitimate violence that outlaws regional traditions, drafts people against their will, takes them to court, jails them if they run away . . . 'You have ordered and commanded so much that there is nothing left to be ordered or commanded', complains the representative of Nordstetten to a county judge in the story 'Good government': 'and you will end up by putting a policeman under every tree to keep it from quarrelling with the wind and drinking too much when it rains'.[6] Here, even rivals in love—gamekeepers, soldiers, land surveyors—belong to repressive bodies.

The formation of nation-states entailed a conflict between national and local loyalties, wrote Charles Tilly, and here it is: the local loyalty towards an older, smaller homeland stubbornly resisting its integration into the Germany to come. *Heimat* against *Vaterland*; the collective rituals so dear to Auerbach (and Mitford); *our* village; *our* society (the title of the first chapter of *Cranford*, Elizabeth Gaskell's village collection, whose last word is *us*). 'To be authorized to say *we*!', exclaims Mitford in 'A country cricket match'; and if one traces the

---

[6] Then, more threateningly: '"You want to take everything from us: now, there happens to be one thing our minds are made up to hold on to." Raising his axe and gnashing his teeth he continued: "And if I must split every door between me and the king with this very axe, I will not give it out of my hand. From time immemorial it is our right to carry axes".'

diffusion of this pronoun in 19th-century culture, two forms—two *rival* forms of collective identity—immediately stand out from the rest: village stories, and national anthems.[7] That the local form leans towards the more proximate and 'inclusive' form (we as I + you), and the national anthem towards the more martial, 'exclusive' one (we as I + they *versus* you: war, enemy, glory . . .), is the apt final touch to their symbolic opposition.

In their animosity towards national centralization, village stories diverge sharply from the provincial novels with which they are often confused, and are, if anything, much closer to regional novels—as is clear in Auerbach's explicit conjunction (*Village* stories of the *Black Forest*), or later in Hardy. 'The region is a place in itself', writes Ian Duncan, 'the source of its own terms of meaning and identity . . . while the province is defined by its difference from [the capital].'[8] Exactly: village and region are alternative homelands of sorts, whereas the provinces embody the capitulation of local reality to the national centre—Emma Bovary's idea that life is *'quelque chose de sublime'* in Paris (or Madrid, or Moscow), and a desert everywhere

[7] Of twenty-eight European anthems I have been able to check, twenty-two establish a significant semantic field around the first person plural, beginning of course with the very first word—*Allons*—of the greatest of them all. Nothing seems as essential to national anthems as this grammatical sign of collective identity; even the name of the country receives fewer mentions (20), while the semantic field of 'glory' has 19, 'past' and 'war' 15, 'enemy' and 'nature' 13, and 'God' a mere 12. Interestingly enough, the three European anthems older than the *Marseillaise*—the Dutch, English, and Danish anthems: 'William of Nassau', 'God Save the Queen', and 'King Christian'—all foreground the figure of the sovereign, and show no interest in the first person plural (except for 'God Save the Queen', which however places it in the object position: 'long to reign over us', 'God save us all', 'may she defend our laws'). The difference between a dynastic and a collective basis for national identity is beautifully captured by this grammatical detail.
[8] Ian Duncan, 'The Provincial or Regional Novel', in Patrick Brantlinger and William Thesing, eds, *A Companion to the Victorian Novel*, Oxford 2002.

else.[9] Like the *provinciae* of antiquity, subject to Rome but denied full citizenship, the provinces are 'negative' entities, defined by *what is not there*; which also explains, by the way, why one cannot map provincial novels—you cannot map what is not there. It happens, there are un-mappable forms (Christmas stories are another one, for different reasons), and these setbacks, disappointing at first, are actually the sign of a method still in touch with reality: geography is a useful tool, yes, but does not explain *everything*. For that, we have astrology and 'Theory'.

VII

What do literary maps do . . . First, they are a good way to prepare a text for analysis. You choose a unit—walks, lawsuits, luxury goods, whatever—find its occurrences, place them in space . . . or in other words: you *reduce* the text to a few elements, and *abstract* them from the narrative flow, and construct a new, *artificial* object like the maps that I have been discussing. And with a little luck, these maps will be *more than the sum of their parts*: they will possess 'emerging' qualities, which were not visible at the lower level. Everybody, from the first readers onwards, had noticed the country walks of *Our Village*; but no one had ever reflected on the circular pattern they project on the English countryside, because no one—in the absence of a map of the book—had ever managed to actually *see* it. Not that the map is itself an explanation, of course: but at least, it offers a model of the

---

[9] If London does not enjoy the same mythical status as other European capitals, the reason is probably that the English provinces were more self-confident than their continental counterparts, especially after 'their' industrial revolution (Manchester, Birmingham, Leeds, Sheffield . . .). The hollow sense of unreality of Emma Bovary, or Ana de Ozores, or the three Prozorov sisters is thus hard to imagine in places like Milton or Middlemarch: full of problems, to be sure, but where life is absolutely real.

narrative universe which rearranges its components in a non-trivial way, and may bring some hidden patterns to the surface.

And patterns are indeed what I have been discussing throughout this chapter. But are they also the proper object of geographical study? In an intelligent critique of the *Atlas of the European Novel*, the Italian geographer Claudio Cerreti has questioned this assumption, pointing out how patterns entail a Cartesian reduction of space to extension, where 'objects are analysed in terms of reciprocal positions and distances . . . whether they are close or far from each other or from something else'. This however is not really geography, Cerreti goes on, but rather *geometry*; and the figures of the *Atlas*, for their part, are not really maps, but diagrams. The diagrams *look* like maps, yes, because they have been 'superimposed on a cartographic plane': but their true nature emerges unmistakably from the way I analyse them, which disregards the specificity of the various locations, to focus almost entirely on their mutual relations; which is indeed the way to read diagrams, but certainly not maps.[10]

Let me give you an instance of what Cerreti means. Figure 22, reproduced from the *Atlas*, is a map of young protagonists of Parisian novels, and of their objects of desire; and I remember the little epiphany I had in front of this figure, when I realized that most young men live on one side of the Seine, and their lovers on the opposite side (or in the separate world of the Faubourg St-Germain). The epiphany, in other words, was *Paris as diagram*:[11] a matrix of relations, not a cluster of individual locations. I could see that the young men were in the Latin Quarter, of course, and the women in the crescent from the

---

[10] Claudio Cerreti, *Bollettino della Società Geografica Italiana*, 1998, pp. 141–8.
[11] Or better, again, as a succession of diagrams (figures 46abcd in the *Atlas*): first, where the young men settle; second, what they desire; third, where they indulge in their fantasies; fourth, where they end up. Each map photographed a particular stage in the plot. *Atlas of the European Novel*, London 1998, pp. 96–9.

FIGURE 22: *Protagonists of Parisian novels, and objects of their desire*

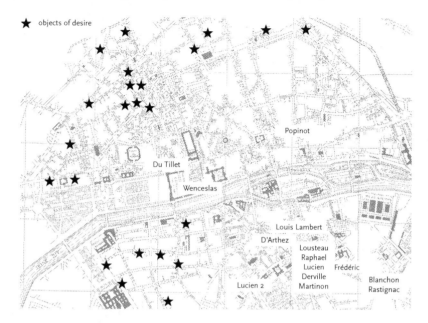

Faubourg St-Germain to the Chaussée d'Antin, and I accounted for it; but without enthusiasm. These specific positions seemed to be the premise of cartography, more than its result. Locations *as such* did not seem that significant, if compared to the *relations* that the map had revealed among them.

Relations among locations as more significant than locations as such . . . But for geography, locations as such *are* significant; geography is not just 'extension' (Cerreti again), but 'intension' too: 'the *quality* of a given space . . . the stratification of *intrinsically different qualities* and heterogeneous phenomena': the Latin Quarter *as Latin Quarter*, in other words, and not only in its opposition to the Chaussée d'Antin. And he is right, of course, and the reason I kept 'forgetting' geography for geometry was, first of all, ignorance: in order to write the

Atlas I had studied some cartography, but had learned it only up to a point, and so I made mistakes. True. But if the *Atlas* is full of diagrams—and, in fact, so is this chapter: where I decided not even to 'superimpose' them onto geographic maps to make the point absolutely clear—if I keep making diagrams, then, it is because for me *geometry 'signifies' more than geography.*[12] More, in the sense that a geometrical pattern is too orderly a shape to be the product of chance. It is a sign that something is at work here—that something has *made* the pattern the way it is.

But what?

VIII

'The form of any portion of matter, whether it be living or dead', writes D'Arcy Thompson in his strange wonderful book *On Growth and Form*, 'may in all cases alike be described as due to the action of force. In short, the form of an object is a "diagram of forces" . . .'[13]

---

[12] Geometry signifies *more* than geography: but it seldom signifies *by itself*. Here, the choice of village stories as the basis of this theoretical sketch may have been unfortunate, as the isotropic space which is so typical of this genre tends to overemphasize the role of geometry at the expense of geography: a fact I became aware of only after long, detailed exchanges with Claudio Cerreti and Jacques Lévy (who have all my gratitude, and shouldn't be held in the least responsible for the views I am expressing). In fact, the most common type of literary map (in the *Atlas of the European Novel*, at any rate) looks less like those of *Our Village* than like that of Parisian novels, where the geometrical pattern is distorted by the specificity of Paris's social geography—as is particularly clear in the case of those three characters who start on the 'wrong' side of the Seine. (For two of them, Du Tillet and Popinot, the explanation is simple: they belong to the space of trade rather than to that of intellectual life in the Latin Quarter; for the third character, Wenceslas, I cannot find a satisfying reason.)

[13] D'Arcy Wentworth Thompson, *On Growth and Form* [1942], Mineola, NY 1992, p. 16.

Diagram: Cartesian space. But diagram *of forces*. The distribution of events between the Black Forest villages and the administrative towns is the diagram of a conflict between local forces and national ones; Mitford's rings, the result of the village's gravitational pull over her perambulating narrator; Balzac's divided Paris, the battle-field between old wealth and ambitious petty bourgeois youth. Each pattern is a clue—a fingerprint of history, almost. 'The form of an object is a "diagram of forces", in this sense, at least, that from it we can . . . deduce the forces that . . . have acted upon it'. Deducing from the *form* of an object the *forces* that have been at work: this is the most elegant definition ever of what literary sociology should be. And for D'Arcy Thompson these forces are of two basic kinds: internal, and external. 'The structure in its final form is, as it were, the inner nucleus molded in various ways by the characteristics of the outer element', wrote Goethe in one of those morphological studies which D'Arcy Thompson knew very well: 'it is precisely thus that the animal retains its viability in the outer world: it is shaped from without as well as from within.'[14]

Shaped from without, as well as from within . . . But so is narrative. On this, the five volumes of *Our Village* offer a splendid test case. In the 1824 volume, remember, the village was the undisputed centre of the surrounding countryside: the centripetal effects of the force 'from within' were omnipresent, while the force 'from without' was nowhere to be seen: the narrator moved freely in every direction in her little idyllic world, and then turned back for the sheer pleasure of returning home, without ever being constrained by a contrary force (like, say, Jude Fawley at Christminster, where he's brutally forced back into Wessex). 'Anything that embodies itself with some freedom seeks a rounded shape', reads another of Goethe's aphorisms, and

[14] Johann Wolfgang von Goethe, 'Toward a General Comparative Theory', 1790–94, in *Scientific Studies*, Princeton 1995, p. 55.

the rounded shape of figure 14 was indeed the embodiment of a literary form—a *mentalité*, an ideology—for which village life was still fundamentally independent of external forces.

This, in 1824. Two collections later, in 1828 (figure 23), the village's gravitational field is already weaker: the walks are less frequent, and their pattern has become wider, less regular; fewer stories take place in the village itself, while several are set outside of Berkshire, in undefined distant towns (and often in the past as well). Something is

FIGURE 23: *Mary Mitford,* Our Village, *volume III [1828]*

wrong with the force from within, but as no counter-force challenges it yet, the basic pattern, although somewhat unsteady, remains in place. But by 1832, it's all over (figure 24): the village's centripetal force is reduced to nothing, and the bulk of the book moves away, thirty miles, sixty, more, to play dumb parlour games in the mansions of the elite (and, again, ever more frequently in the past).

FIGURE 24: *Mary Mitford,* Our Village, *volume v [1832]*

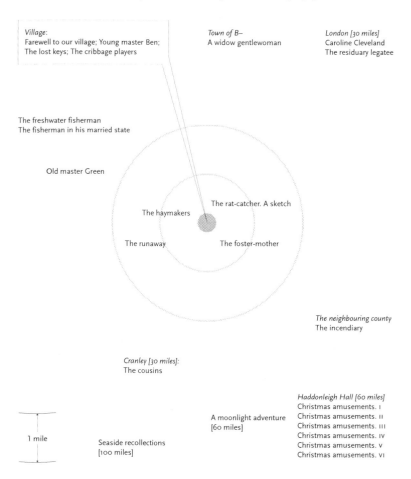

Village:
Farewell to our village; Young master Ben;
The lost keys; The cribbage players

Town of B–
A widow gentlewoman

London [30 miles]
Caroline Cleveland
The residuary legatee

The freshwater fisherman
The fisherman in his married state

Old master Green

The haymakers

The rat-catcher. A sketch

The runaway

The foster-mother

The neighbouring county
The incendiary

Cranley [30 miles]:
The cousins

Haddonleigh Hall [60 miles]
Christmas amusements. I
Christmas amusements. II
A moonlight adventure   Christmas amusements. III
[60 miles]   Christmas amusements. IV
Christmas amusements. V
Seaside recollections   Christmas amusements. VI
[100 miles]

1 mile

FIGURE 25: *Luddism, 1811–12, and Captain Swing disturbances, 1830*

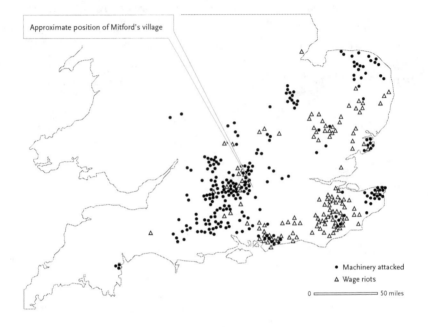

Source: John Langton and R. J. Morris, eds, *Atlas of Industrializing Britain*

Something has happened, here, and two stories suggest what it is: rick-burning. 'Oh the horror of those fires—breaking forth night after night, sudden, yet expected . . .' reads the first narrative of the volume, 'The incendiary'; 'We lived in the midst of the disturbed districts,' adds 'Young master Ben', and 'no one who lived within reach of the armed peasantry . . . could get rid of the vague idea of danger which might arrive at any moment . . .'. The armed peasantry of the 1830 uprisings (figure 25): this is the 'force from without' which has 'acted upon' *Our Village*, altering its narrative pattern beyond recognition. Figure 26, which charts the three volumes one next to the other, summarizes the disintegration of Mitford's chronotope.

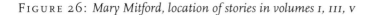

FIGURE 26: *Mary Mitford, location of stories in volumes I, III, V*

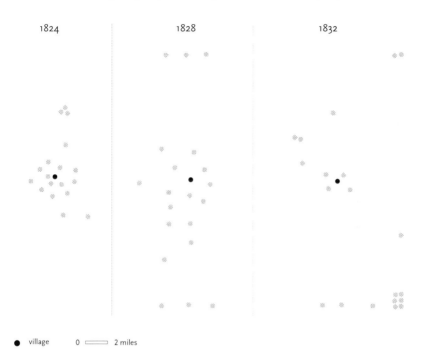

1824   1828   1832

● village   0 ⊏⊐ 2 miles

In a very large part of morphology, our essential task lies in the comparison of related forms rather than in the precise definition of each; and the deformation of a complicated figure may be a phenomenon easy of comprehension, though the figure itself have to be left unanalysed and undefined . . . The essential condition is, that the form of the entire structure under investigation should be found to vary in a more or less uniform manner.

D'Arcy Thompson,
On Growth and Form

IX

Let me conclude by briefly returning to the beginning. Thomas Moule's 1837 map of Berkshire, reproduced in figure 13, gave a good idea of the type of geography congenial to modern idyllic form: parks, rivers, country seats, low urbanization (and no railway in the early twenties, when Mitford starts writing). Figure 27 is another of Moule's maps, Cheshire this time, and Knutsford, near the centre of the figure, is Gaskell's 'Cranford', the setting of her 1853 rewriting of *Our Village*. In this case, Moule's map *precedes* the novel by fifteen years, but it already casts a shadow over Gaskell's projected idyll: urbanization is higher, Manchester is just 15 miles away, and by an uncanny coincidence Mitford's typical walk would end more or less at the Grand Junction Railway, where one of the book's most sympathetic characters, distracted by the latest number of *Pickwick*—the

FIGURE 27: *Cranford*

Source: Moule, *The English Counties Delineated*

regular novelty which has just arrived from London—is killed by a train. Social geography does not agree with the form of the idyll here, and in order to keep the genre alive Gaskell must literally hibernate her village: Cranford is presented as a place under siege, hardly alive, where no one dares to go anywhere, and everything is painstakingly saved (candles, carpets, clothes, stories . . .) to make it last as long as possible; and even so, only the half-magic arrival of Indian wealth can prolong its artificial existence. For every genre comes a moment when its inner form can no longer represent the most significant aspects of contemporary reality, I wrote in the previous chapter: at which point, either the genre loses its form under the impact of reality, thereby disintegrating, or it betrays reality in the name of form, becoming, in Shklovsky's words, a 'dull epigone'. Mitford in 1832, and Gaskell twenty years later, are the two ends of the spectrum: *Our Village* explodes, and *Cranford* is Madame Tussaud's idea of a village story.

X

Maps, is the title of this chapter. But there are maps and maps: Moule (figures 13 and 27), Barrell (15–16), Langton and Morris (25) have all made maps of real English spaces, reproducing actual features of their material environment; I have made maps/diagrams of fictional worlds, where the real and the imaginary coexist in varying, often elusive proportions. The figures are different. But when they are collated and juxtaposed, they allow us a glimpse of what D'Arcy Thompson had in mind in his great final chapter on 'The theory of transformations':

> We rise from a conception of form to an understanding of the forces which gave rise to it . . . and in the comparison of kindred forms . . . we discern the magnitude and the direction of the forces which have sufficed to convert the one form into the other.[15]

[15] D'Arcy Thompson, *On Growth and Form*, p. 1027.

In the comparison of the kindred forms of *Our Village* in 1824, 1828, and 1832, and of the initial and final decades of *Annals of the Parish*, and of the British and German village stories, we discern indeed the various directions in which rural class struggle, the industrial take-off, and the process of state formation have 'converted' the shape of nineteenth-century idylls. As in an experiment, the force 'from without' of large national processes alters the initial narrative structure beyond recognition, and reveals the direct, almost tangible relationship between social conflict and literary form. Reveals form as a diagram of forces; or perhaps, even, as *nothing but force.*

Trees

Figure 28 (overleaf) reproduces the only tree—'an odd looking affair, but indispensable', as Darwin writes to his publisher in the spring of 1859[1]—in *The Origin of Species*; it appears in the fourth chapter, 'Natural selection' (which in later editions becomes 'Natural selection; or, the survival of the fittest'), in the section on 'Divergence of character'. But when the image is first introduced, Darwin does not call it a 'tree':[2]

> Now let us see how this principle of great benefit being derived from divergence of character, combined with the principles of natural selection and of extinction, will tend to act. The accompanying diagram will aid us in understanding this rather perplexing subject . . .[3]

[1] 'It is an odd looking affair, but is *indispensable*', continues the letter to John Murray of May 31, 1859, 'to show the nature of the very complex affinities of past & present animals'. Frederick Burkhardt and Sydney Smith, eds, *The Correspondence of Charles Darwin*, vol. VII (1858–59), Cambridge 1991, p. 300.
[2] The word 'tree' appears only at the end of the chapter, and surrounded by signs of hesitation, possibly because of the religious echoes associated with the Tree of Life: 'The affinities of all the beings of the same class have *sometimes* been represented by a great tree. I *believe* this simile *largely* speaks the truth': Charles Darwin, *The Origin of Species*, 1859; facsimile of the first edition, Cambridge, MA 2001, p. 129 (italics mine).
[3] Darwin, *Origin*, p. 116.

FIGURE 28: *Divergence of character*

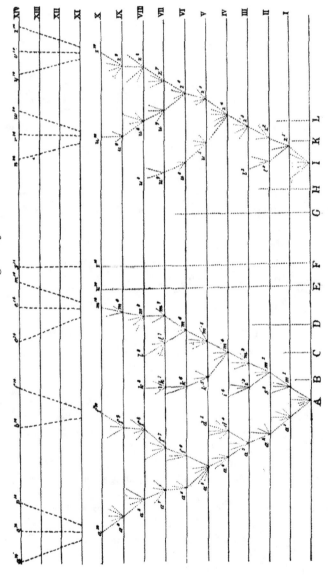

Let A be a common, widely-diffused, and varying species, belonging to a genus large in its own country. The little fan of diverging dotted lines of unequal lengths proceeding from A may represent its varying offspring . . . Only those variations which are in some way profitable will be preserved or naturally selected. And here the importance of the principle of benefit being derived from divergence of character comes in; for this will generally lead to the most different or divergent variations (represented by the outer dotted lines) being preserved and accumulated by natural selection.

Charles Darwin, *On the Origin of Species*

Diagram, again. After the quantitative diagrams of the first chapter, and the spatial ones of the second, evolutionary trees constitute *morphological* diagrams, where history is systematically correlated with form. And indeed, in contrast to literary studies—where theories of form are usually blind to history, and historical work blind to form—for evolutionary thought morphology and history are truly the two dimensions of the same tree: where the vertical axis charts, from the bottom up, the regular passage of time (every interval, writes Darwin, 'one thousand generations'), while the horizontal one follows the formal diversification ('the little fans of diverging dotted lines') that will eventually lead to 'well-marked varieties', or to entirely new species.

The horizontal axis follows formal diversification . . . But Darwin's words are stronger: he speaks of 'this rather perplexing subject'— elsewhere, 'perplexing & unintelligible'[4]—whereby forms don't just 'change', but change by always *diverging* from each other (remember, we are in the section on 'Divergence of Character').[5] Whether as a result of historical accidents, then, or under the action of a specific

[4] 'You will find Ch. IV perplexing & unintelligible', he writes to Lyell on September 2, 1859, 'without the aid of enclosed queer Diagram, of which I send old & useless proof': Burkhardt and Smith, eds, *Correspondence of Charles Darwin*, p. 329.
[5] 'The intent of Darwin's famous diagram has almost always been misunderstood', writes Stephen Jay Gould: 'Darwin did not draw this unique diagram simply to illustrate the generality of evolutionary branching, but primarily to explicate the principle of divergence. Darwin's solution . . . holds that natural selection will generally favor the most extreme, the most different, the most divergent forms in a spectrum of variation emanating from any common parental stock. . . . Note how only two species of the original array (A–L) ultimately leave descendants—the left extreme A and the near right extreme I. Note how each diversifying species first generates an upward fan of variants about its modal form, and how only the peripheral populations of the fan survive to diversify further. Note that the total morphospace (horizontal axis) expands by divergence, although only two of the original species leave descendants.' Stephen Jay Gould, *The Structure of Evolutionary Theory*, Cambridge, MA 2002, pp. 228–9, 235–6.

'principle',[6] the reality of divergence pervades the history of life, defining its morphospace—its space-of-forms: an important concept, in the pages that follow—as an intrinsically expanding one.

From a single common origin, to an immense variety of solutions: it is this incessant growing-apart of life forms that the branches of a morphological tree capture with such intuitive force. 'A tree can be viewed *as a simplified description of a matrix of distances*', write Cavalli-Sforza, Menozzi and Piazza in the methodological prelude to their *History and Geography of Human Genes*; and figure 29, with its mirror-like alignment of genetic groups and linguistic families drifting away from each other (in a 'correspondence [that] is remarkably high but not perfect', as they note with aristocratic aplomb),[7] makes clear what they mean: a tree is a way of sketching *how far* a certain language has moved from another one, or from their common point of origin.

And if language evolves by diverging, why not literature too?

I

For Darwin, 'divergence of character' interacts throughout history with 'natural selection and extinction': as variations grow apart from

[6] 'One might say . . . that "divergence of character" requires no separate principle beyond adaptation, natural selection, and historical contingency . . . Climates alter; topography changes; populations become isolated, and some, adapting to modified environments, form new species. What more do we need? . . . But Darwin grew dissatisfied with a theory that featured a general principle to explain adaptation, but then relied upon historical accidents of changing environments to resolve diversity. He decided that a fully adequate theory of evolution required an equally strong principle of diversity, one that acted intrinsically and predictably': Gould, *Structure*, p. 226.
[7] Luigi Luca Cavalli-Sforza, Paolo Menozzi and Alberto Piazza, *The History and Geography of Human Genes*, Princeton 1994, pp. 38, 99 (italics mine).

FIGURE 29: *Linguistic trees*

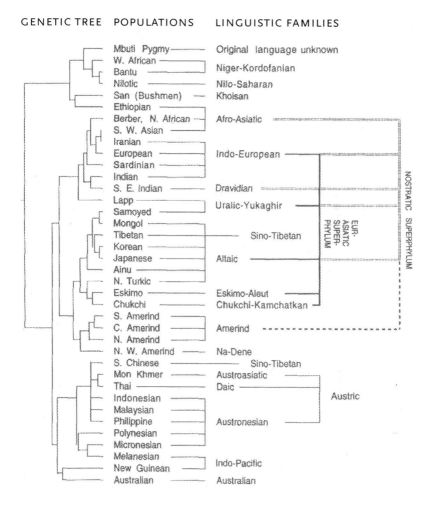

Why is there a close similarity between linguistic and genetic trees? . . . The correlation is certainly not due to the effect of genes on languages; if anything, it is likely that there is a reverse influence, in that linguistic barriers may strengthen the genetic isolation between groups speaking different languages . . . The explanation of the parallelism between genetic and linguistic trees is to be sought in the common effect of . . . events determining the separation of two groups. After fission and migration of one or both moieties to a different area, they are partially or completely isolated from each other. Reciprocal isolation causes both genetic and linguistic differentiation.

L. Luca Cavalli-Sforza, Paolo Menozzi and Alberto Piazza, *The History and Geography of Human Genes*

each other, selection intervenes, allowing only a few to survive. In a seminar of a few years ago, I addressed the analogous problem of literary survival, using as a test case the early stages of British detective fiction. We chose clues as the trait whose transformations were likely to be most revealing for the history of the genre, and proceeded to chart the relationships between Arther Conan Doyle and some of his contemporaries as a series of branchings, which added up to the (modest) tree of figure 30.[8]

Here, from the very first branching at the bottom of the tree (whether clues were present or not) two things were immediately clear: the 'formal' fact that several of Doyle's rivals (those on the left) did not use clues—and the 'historical' fact that they were all forgotten. It is a good illustration of what the literary market is like: ruthless competition—hinging on form. Readers discover that they like a certain device, and if a story doesn't seem to include it, they simply don't read it (and the story becomes extinct). This pressure of cultural selection probably explains the second branching of the tree, where clues *are* present, but serve no real function: as in 'Race with the Sun', for instance, where a clue reveals to the hero that the drug is in the third cup of coffee, and then, when he is offered the third cup, he actually *drinks it*. Which is indeed 'perplexing & unintelligible', and the only possible explanation is that these writers realized that clues were popular, and tried to smuggle them into their stories—but hadn't really understood *how* clues worked, and so didn't use them very well.

---

[8] I am here summarizing and updating the results of a larger study, 'The Slaughterhouse of Literature', *Modern Language Quarterly*, March 2000. It should however be kept in mind that a process of selection determined by a *single character*, like the one presented here, is almost certainly atypical: it is (hopefully) valid for detective fiction, given the centrality of clues within its narrative structure—but it is precisely this 'condensation' of the structure in a single element that is highly unusual. As a rule, literary trees will have to be based on a multiplicity of morphological traits.

FIGURE 30: *Presence of clues and the genesis of detective fiction*

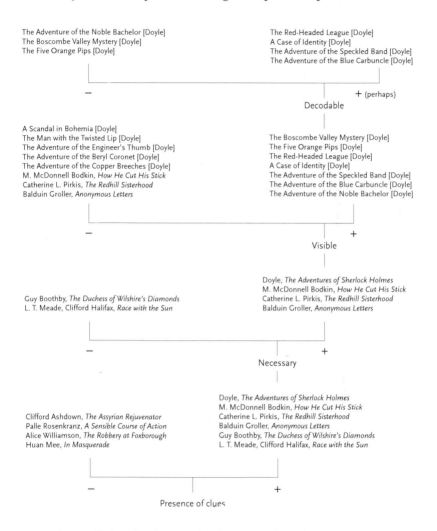

From the standpoint of technique, the devices employed by Conan Doyle in his stories are simpler than the devices we find in other English mystery novels. On the other hand, they show greater concentration . . . The most important clues take the form of secondary facts, which are presented in such a way that the reader does not notice them . . . they are intentionally placed in the oblique form of a subordinate clause . . . on which the storyteller does not dwell.

Viktor Shklovsky, *Theory of Prose*

Third branching: clues are present, they have a function, but are not visible: the detective mentions them in his final explanation, but we have never 'seen' them in the course of the story. Here we lose the last of Doyle's rivals (which is exactly what, sooner or later, we had expected to see), but we also lose half of the *Adventures of Sherlock Holmes*, which we hadn't expected at all; and the next branching—clues must be not just visible, but decodable by the reader: soon to become a key 'technical law' of the genre—is even more surprising, since decodable clues appear, even being generous, in only four of the twelve *Adventures* and, being strict, in none of them.

Why this last-minute stumble on Doyle's part? I try to explain it in 'The Slaughterhouse of Literature', and will not repeat the argument here. But I will mention an objection raised in the course of the seminar to the logic behind figure 30. This tree, said one of the participants, assumes that morphology is the key factor of literary history: that Doyle owes his phenomenal success to his greater skill in the handling of clues; to his being the only one who made it to the top of the tree, as it were. But why should form be the decisive reason for survival? Why not social privilege instead—the fact that Doyle was writing for a well-established magazine, and his rivals were not?

Plausible. So I went to the library, where I discovered that, in the course of the 1890s, over one hundred detective stories by twenty-five different authors had been published in the *Strand Magazine* alongside Sherlock Holmes. Since so many writers had access to the same venue as Doyle, the 'social privilege' objection lost its force; but, more importantly, the study of those hundred-odd stories—while confirming the uniqueness of Doyle's technical feat—also added two entirely new branches to the initial tree of detective fiction (figure 31). The more one looked in the archive, in other words, the more complex and 'darwinian' became the genre's morphospace. The family of narrative forms evoked in the first of these chapters was beginning to take shape.

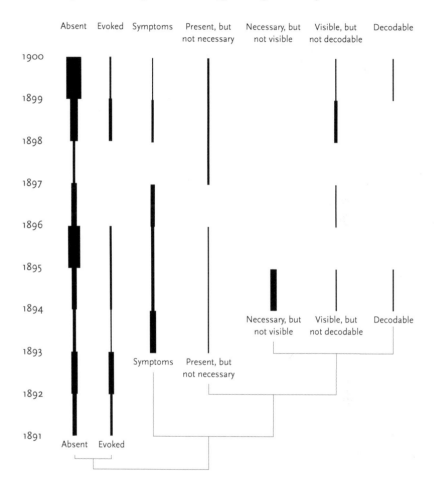

In this diagram, where the thickness of the line indicates the number of stories published during each year, the two new branches are the second and third from the left. The former includes those stories in which clues are not present, but are verbally evoked, or perhaps invoked by the characters ('If only we had a clue!'; 'Did you find any clues?'), in what is probably another awkward attempt to smuggle them into a text that does not really need them. In the third branch from the left, clues are present, but always in the form of medical symptoms, as if in homage to the old art of medical semiotics—which had of course been Doyle's model from the very start: Holmes is modelled on Edinburgh's Dr Bell, has always a doctor at his side, studies his clients as if they were patients, etc.

II

Is divergence a factor, in literary history? These first findings suggest a cautious Yes. But what is it, that generates this morphological drifting-away? Texts? I doubt it. Texts are distributed on the branches of the tree, yes, but the 'nodes' of the branching process are not defined by texts here, but by clues (their absence, presence, visibility etc): by something that is much *smaller* than any individual text—a sentence, a metaphor ('It was the band! The speckled band!'), at times ('I could only catch some allusion to a rat') not even a full word. And on the other hand, this system of differences at the microscopic level adds up to something that is much *larger* than any individual text, and which in our case is of course the genre—or the tree—of detective fiction.

The very small, and the very large; these are the forces that shape literary history. Devices and genres; not texts. Texts are certainly the *real objects* of literature (in the *Strand Magazine* you don't find 'clues' or 'detective fiction', you find *Sherlock Holmes*, or *Hilda Wade*, or *The Adventures of a Man of Science*); but they are not the right *objects of knowledge* for literary history. Take the concept of genre: usually, literary criticism approaches it in terms of what Ernst Mayr calls 'typological thinking':[9] we choose a 'representative individual', and through it define the genre as a whole. *Sherlock Holmes*, say, and detective fiction; *Wilhelm Meister* and the *Bildungsroman*; you analyse Goethe's novel, and it counts as an analysis of the entire genre, because for typological thinking there is really no gap between the real object and the object of knowledge. But once a genre is visualized *as a tree*, the continuity between the two inevitably disappears: the genre becomes an abstract 'diversity spectrum' (Mayr again), whose internal multiplicity no individual text will ever be able to represent. And so, even 'A Scandal in Bohemia' becomes just one leaf among many: delightful, of course—but no longer entitled to stand for the genre as a whole.

[9] See Ernst Mayr, *Populations, Species and Evolution*, Cambridge, MA 1970; *Evolution and the Diversity of Life*, Cambridge, MA 1976; and *Toward a New Philosophy of Biology*, Cambridge, MA 1988.

A diversity spectrum. Quite wide, in figures 30 and 31, because when a new genre first arises, and no 'central' convention has yet crystallized, its space-of-forms is usually open to the most varied experiments. And then, there is the pressure of the market. The twenty-five authors of the *Strand Magazine* are all competing for the same, limited market niche, and their meanderings through morphospace have probably a lot to do with a keen desire to outdo each other's inventions: after all, when mystery writers come up with an 'aeronaut' who kills a hiker with the anchor of his balloon, or a somnambulist painter who draws the face of the man he has murdered, or a chair that catapults its occupants into a neighboring park, they are clearly looking for the Great Idea that will seal their success. And yet, just as clearly, aeronauts and cata- pults are totally *random* attempts at innovation, in the sense in which evolutionary theory uses the term: they show no foreknowledge—no idea, really—of what may be good for literary survival. In making writ- ers branch out in every direction, then, the market also pushes them into all sorts of crazy blind alleys; and divergence becomes indeed, as Darwin had seen, inseparable from extinction.

There are many ways of being alive, writes Richard Dawkins, but many more ways of being dead—and figures 30 and 31, with all those texts that were so quickly forgotten, fully bear out his point: literary pathology, one may almost call it. But instead of reiterating the verdict of the market, abandoning extinct literature to the oblivion decreed by its initial readers, these trees take the lost 99 per cent of the archive and reintegrate it into the fabric of literary history, allowing us to finally 'see' it. It is the same issue raised in the first chapter—the one per cent of the canon, and the ninety-nine of forgotten literature—but viewed from a different angle: whereas graphs abolish all qualitative difference among their data, trees try to *articulate* that difference. In the graph of British novels between 1710 and 1850, for instance (figure 14), *Pride and Prejudice* and *The Life of Pill Garlick; Rather a Whimsical Sort of Fellow*, appear as exactly alike: two dots in the 1813 column, impossible to tell apart. But figures 30 and 31 aim pre- cisely at *distinguishing* 'The Red-Headed League' from 'The Assyrian

Rejuvenator' and 'How He Cut His Stick', thus establishing an intelligible relationship between canonical and non-canonical branches.

III

Trees; or, divergence in literary history. But this view of culture usually encounters a very explicit objection. 'Among the many differences in deep principle between natural evolution and cultural change', writes Stephen Jay Gould, their 'topology'—that is to say, the abstract overall shape of the two processes—is easily the most significant:

> Darwinian evolution at the species level and above is a story of continuous and irreversible proliferation . . . a process of constant separation and distinction. Cultural change, on the other hand, receives a powerful boost from amalgamation and anastomosis of different traditions. A clever traveller may take one look at a foreign wheel, import the invention back home, and change his local culture fundamentally and forever.[10]

The traveller and his wheel are not a great example (they are a case of simple diffusion, not of amalgamation), but the general point is clear, and is frequently made by historians of technology. George Basalla:

> Different biological species usually do not interbreed, and on the rare occasions when they do their offspring are infertile. Artifactual types, on the other hand, are routinely combined to produce new and fruitful entities . . . The internal combustion engine branch was joined with that of the bicycle and horse-drawn carriage to create the automobile branch, which in turn merged with the dray wagon to produce the motor truck.[11]

Artifactual species combined in new and fruitful entities: in support of his thesis, Basalla reproduces Alfred Kroeber's ingenious 'tree of culture' (figure 32), whose Alice-in-Wonderland quality makes the reality of

[10] Stephen Jay Gould, *Full House. The Spread of Excellence from Plato to Darwin*, New York 1996, pp. 220–1.
[11] George Basalla, *The Evolution of Technology*, Cambridge 1988, pp. 137–8.

FIGURE 32: *Tree of Culture*

THE TREE OF LIFE AND THE TREE OF THE KNOWLEDGE OF
GOOD AND EVIL—THAT IS, OF HUMAN CULTURE

The course of organic evolution can be portrayed properly as a tree of life, as Darwin has called it, with trunk, limbs, branches, and twigs. The course of development of human culture in history cannot be so described, even metaphorically. There is a constant branching-out, but the branches also grow together again, wholly or partially, all the time. Culture diverges, but it syncretizes and anastomoses too. Life really does nothing but diverge: its occasional convergences are superficial resemblances, not a joining or a reabsorption. A branch on the tree of life may approach another branch; it will not normally coalesce with it. The tree of culture, on the contrary, is a ramification of such coalescences, assimilations, or acculturations. This schematic diagram visualizes this contrast.

Alfred Kroeber, *Anthropology*

convergence unforgettably clear. As it should be, because convergence is indeed a major factor of cultural evolution. But is it *the only one?*

'*Culture diverges*, but it syncretizes and anastomoses too', runs Kroeber's comment to the tree of culture; and Basalla: 'the oldest surviving made things . . . stand at the beginning of the *interconnected, branching,* continuous series of artifacts shaped by deliberate human effort'. Interconnected *and* branching; syncretism *and* divergence: rather than irreconcilable 'differences in deep principle' between convergence and divergence, passages like these (which could be easily multiplied) suggest a sort of division of labour between them; or perhaps, better, a cycle to which they both contribute in turn. Convergence, I mean, only arises *on the basis of previous divergence*, and its power tends in fact to be directly proportional to the distance between the original branches (bicycles, and internal combustion engines). Conversely, a successful convergence usually produces *a powerful new burst of divergence*: like the 'new evolutionary series [which] began almost immediately after Whitney's [cotton gin] was put to work', and which quickly became, concludes Basalla, 'the point of origin for an entirely new set of artifacts'.[12]

Divergence prepares the ground for convergence, which unleashes further divergence: this seems to be the typical pattern.[13] Moreover, the force of the two mechanisms varies widely from field to field, ranging from the pole of technology, where convergence is particularly strong, to the opposite extreme of language, where divergence—remember the 'matrix of distances' of figure 29—is clearly the dominant factor; while the specific position of literature—this technology-of-language— within the whole spectrum remains to be determined.[14] And don't be

---

[12] Basalla, *The Evolution of Technology*, pp. 30, 34.

[13] It is easy (in theory, at least) to envision how this cyclical matrix could be applied to the history of genres: convergence among separate lineages would be decisive in the genesis of genres of particular significance; then, once a genre's form stabilizes, 'interbreeding' would stop, and divergence would become the dominant force.

[14] In Thomas Pavel's recent *La pensée du roman*, Paris 2003, which is the most ambitious theory of the novel since the masterpieces of the inter-war years, divergence is the fundamental force during the first seventeen centuries of the novel's existence, and convergence in the last three (these are my extrapolations, not Pavel's). The interpretation of these results is however far from obvious. Should one insist on the striking quantitative supremacy of divergence even in the notoriously 'synchretic' genre of the novel? Or should one focus on the (apparent) historical trend, viewing divergence as a 'primitive' morphological principle, and convergence as a more 'mature' one? And are Balzac, say, or Joyce, only instances of convergence (pp. 245, 373)—or are they also the initiators of strikingly new formal branches? All questions for another occasion.

misled by the 'topological' technicalities of all this: the real content of the controversy, not technical at all, is our very idea of culture. Because if the basic mechanism of change is that of divergence, then cultural history is bound to be random, full of false starts, and profoundly path-dependent: a direction, once taken, can seldom be reversed, and culture hardens into a true 'second nature'—hardly a benign metaphor. If, on the other hand, the basic mechanism is that of convergence, change will be frequent, fast, deliberate, reversible: culture becomes more plastic, more *human*, if you wish. But as human history is so seldom human, this is perhaps not the strongest of arguments.

IV

One last tree: this time, not the 'many more ways of being dead' of Doyle's rivals, but the still numerous 'ways of being alive' discovered between 1800 and 2000 by that great narrative device known as 'free indirect style'. The technique was first noticed in an article on French grammar published in 1887 in the *Zeitschrift für romanische Philologie*, which described it, in passing, as 'a peculiar mix of indirect and direct discourse, which draws the verbal tenses and pronouns from the former, and the tone and the order of the sentence from the latter'.[15] Here is an example from *Mansfield Park*:

> It was the abode of noise, disorder, and impropriety. Nobody was in their right place, nothing was done as it ought to be. She could not respect her parents, as she had hoped.[16]

Nobody was *in their right place*, nothing was done *as it ought to be*: the tone is clearly Fanny's, and expresses her profound emotional frustration at her parents' house. Nobody *was* in their right place . . .

---

[15] A. Tobler, 'Vermischte Beiträge zur französischen Grammatik', *Zeitschrift für romanische Philologie*, 1887, p. 437.
[16] *Mansfield Park*, ch. 39.

She could not respect *her* parents: the (past) verbal tenses and (third person) pronouns evoke for their part the typical distance of narrative discourse. Emotions, plus distance: it is truly a peculiar mix, free indirect style, but its composite nature was precisely what made it 'click' with that other strange compromise formation which is the process of modern socialization: by leaving the individual voice a certain amount of freedom, while permeating it with the impersonal stance of the narrator, free indirect style enacted that *véritable transposition de l'objectif dans le subjectif* [17] which is indeed the substance of the socialization process. And the result was the genesis of an unprecedented 'third' voice, intermediate and almost neutral in tone between character and narrator: the composed, slightly resigned voice of the *well-socialized individual*, of which Austen's heroines—these young women who speak of themselves *in the third person*, as if from the outside—are such stunning examples. [18]

Placed as it is halfway between social *doxa* and the individual voice, free indirect style is a good indicator of their changing balance of forces, of which the tree in figure 33 (overleaf) offers a schematic visualization. And as can be seen, not much happens as long as free indirect style remains confined to western Europe; at most, we have the gradual, entropic drift from 'reflective' to 'non-reflective' consciousness: [19] that is to say, from sharp punctual utterances like those in *Mansfield Park*, to Flaubert's all-encompassing moods, where the character's inner space is unknowingly colonized by the commonplaces of

[17] Charles Bally, 'Le style indirecte libre en français moderne', *Germanisch-Romanische Monatschrift*, 1912, second part, p. 603.
[18] I have analysed in detail the connexion between free indirect style and socialization in 'Il secolo serio', *Il romanzo*, vol. 1, Torino 2001 (forthcoming, Princeton 2005). Needless to say, I do not claim that free indirect style is *only* used to represent the process of socialization (which would be absurd), but rather that between the two existed—especially early on—a profound elective affinity.
[19] For these terms, see Ann Banfield's classic study of free indirect style, *Unspeakable Sentences*, Boston 1982.

public opinion. But just as the individual mind seems about to be submerged by ideology, a geographical shift to the east reverses the trend, associating free indirect style with conflict rather than with consensus. Raskolnikov's inner speech, writes Bakhtin

> is filled with other people's words that he has recently heard or read [and is] constructed like a succession of living and impassioned replies to all those words . . . He does not think about phenomena, he speaks with them . . . he addresses himself (often in the second person singular, as if to another person), he tries to persuade himself, he taunts, exposes, ridicules himself .[20]

A language filled with 'other people's words', just like Emma Bovary's: but where those words, instead of being passively echoed, arouse 'living and impassioned replies'. Or to quote the passage chosen by Bakhtin himself to illustrate his point (it's the moment when Raskolnikov reacts to the news of his sister's impending marriage):

> 'Won't take place? And what are you going to do to stop it? Forbid it? By what right? What can you promise them instead, in order to possess such a right? To devote your whole life, your whole future to them, *when you finish your course and get a job*? We've heard that one before, that's just maybe—what about *now*? I mean, you've got to do something right now, do you realize that?' . . . It was a long time since [these questions] had begun to lacerate his heart, and it was positively an age since his present sense of anguish and depression had come into being . . . It was clear that now was not the time to feel miserable, to suffer passively with the thought that the questions were not capable of resolution; no, instead he must do something, and at once, as quickly as possible. Whatever happened, he must take some action, or else . . .[21]

[20] Mikhail Bakhtin, *Problems of Dostoevsky's Poetics*, 1929–63, Minneapolis 1984, pp. 237–8. The dialogic reinterpretation of free indirect style sketched by Bakhtin is extensively developed in Volosinov's chapters on 'quasi-direct discourse' in *Marxism and the Philosophy of Language* [1929], Cambridge, MA 1993, pp. 125–59; see also Gary Morson and Caryl Emerson, *Mikhail Bakhtin. Creation of a Prosaics*, Palo Alto, CA 1990, esp. pp. 343–4.
[21] *Crime and Punishment*, ch. 4.

FIGURE 33: *Free indirect style in modern narrative, 1800–2000*

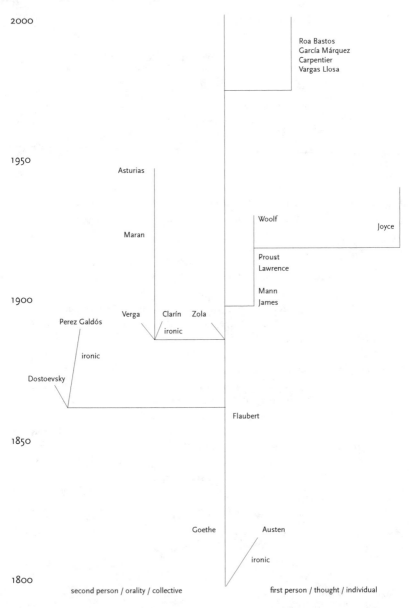

This figure reflects work in progress, and is therefore quite tentative, especially in the case of non-European literatures, and of the diachronic span of the various branches.

Great page. But can we really speak of free indirect style for those sentences in 'the second person singular, as if to another person' that open the passage, and that are so crucial for Bakhtin's argument (and for his entire theory of the novel)? No, not quite: the second person (especially if in quotes) indicates the *direct* discourse of an open-ended discussion, rather than (as in the second half of the passage) the narrative report of thoughts and emotions which is the typical modality of free indirect style. Why this double register, then, in the representation of Raskolnikov's inner debate? Probably, what happened was something like this: once free indirect style 'migrated' into the world of *Crime and Punishment*, it began drifting towards the stylistic centre of gravity of the novel—dialogism—and became as a result much more intense and dramatic than ever before ('it was clear that now was not the time to feel miserable . . .'). It became, one could say, almost dialogic. Almost. But in the end, free indirect style was a *narrative* technique, whose retrospective inflection ruled out the open-endedness of dialogism. And so, after having shuttled back and forth between the two techniques, Dostoevsky toned down free indirect style, so that dialogism could come into its own.

A branch of the tree of life may approach another branch, wrote A. L. Kroeber in the passage quoted a few pages back, but it will not normally coalesce with it. True. And at times, the same is true of the tree of culture: even an extraordinarily flexible technique like free indirect style (and in the hands of a writer of genius) could never 'coalesce' with the branch of dialogism, no matter how close the two styles had come to each other. Culture is not the realm of ubiquitous 'hybridity': it, too, has its barriers, its impassable limits. In a moment, we will encounter another example.

V

Bakhtin's conceptual vocabulary, with its emphasis on the oral threads within novelistic prose, is a good prologue to the next branching of the tree, which occurs around 1880, at the height of the naturalist movement. Here, the fault line—which is, again, geographic and morphological at once—runs between different forms of symbolic hegemony in *fin-de-siècle* Europe: in the West, the silent, interiorized *doxa* of large nation-states, arising almost impersonally from newspapers, books, and an anonymous public opinion; in the South, the noisy, *multi*-personal 'chorus' (Leo Spitzer) of the small village of *I Malavoglia*, or the sharp whispers of the provincial confessionals of *La Regenta*; later, the *longue durée* of collective oral myths in *Batouala* or *Men of Maize*.[22] Here, free indirect style embodies a form of social cohesion which—in its reliance on explicit, *spoken* utterances, rather than 'non-reflective' absorption—is more quarrelsome and intrusive than in western Europe, but also much more unstable: the spokesmen for the social (villagers, confessor, chief) must be always *physically there*, ready to reiterate over and over again the dominant values, or else things fall apart. As indeed they do, in all of these novels.

Another collective voice, of a different nature, echoes in the same years in Zola's *Germinal*: the voice of the working class. The main speaker, at the great nocturnal gathering during the miners' strike:

[22] Two examples. 'Nowadays mischief-makers got up to all kinds of tricks; and at Trezza you saw faces which had never been seen there before, on the cliffs, people claiming to be going fishing, and they even stole the sheets put out to dry, if there happened to be any. Poor Nunziata had had a new sheet stolen that way. Poor girl! Imagine robbing her, a girl who had worked her fingers to the bone to provide bread for all those little brothers her father had left on her hands when he had upped and gone to seek his fortune in Alexandria of Egypt.' Giovanni Verga, *I Malavoglia*, ch. 2.
   'He's a good old man, the sun, and so equitable! He shines for all living people, from the greatest to the most humble. He knows neither rich nor poor, neither black nor white. Whatever may be their colour, whatever may be their fortune, all men are his sons. He loves them all equally; favours their plantations; dispels, to please them, the cold and sullen fog; reabsorbs the rain; and drives out the shadow. Ah! The shadow. Unpityingly, relentlessly, the sun pursues it wherever it may be. He hates nothing else.' René Maran, *Batouala*, ch. 8.

These poor devils, they were just machine-fodder, they were penned like cattle, the big companies were devouring them bit by bit, legalizing slavery . . . But the miner was no longer the ignorant brute buried in the bowels of the earth . . . From the depths of the pit an army was springing up . . . Yes!, labour would call capital to account, this impersonal god, unknown to the worker, crouching somewhere in the mystery of its tabernacle, whence he sucked the blood of the poor starving creatures he lived on![23]

Here, we find all of the elements we have encountered so far. There is the emotional spark (*ces misérables* . . .) that brings free indirect style into being. There is the overlap of character and narrator (with the metaphor of the avenging army that will return, unforgettably, in the last sentence of the novel), and the telescoping of individual and social class, with the 'we' of direct discourse that turns into the third person plural. And then, there is the metamorphosis of popular language into 'French'. Eugen Weber:

French, which prizes abstract terms over concrete ones . . . refines language by eliminating the details that count so much in popular speech and the great variety of specific and descriptive terms that flourished in patois. It prefers to interpret rather than describe reality, to express ideas, not just to relate facts.[24]

Peasants into Frenchmen, is the title of Weber's book; miners into Frenchmen, one could repeat for the free indirect style of *Germinal*, that seems to find a voice for the 'nationalization of the masses' of the late 19th century. Not for nothing, its ideal vehicle is Etienne Lantier, who is at once one of the miners, and their 'representative': the man who has risen from the ranks because he 'speaks well' (and hopes to use his gift to make a career—in Paris, possibly). Class antagonism, although powerfully expressed, bleeds oddly into individual ambition,

---

[23] *Germinal* IV.7.
[24] Eugen Weber, *Peasants into Frenchmen. The Modernization of Rural France 1870–1914*, Stanford 1976, p. 93.

placing free indirect style once again in a position—if not exactly ambiguous—of implicit, and almost invisible, social mediation.

VI

So far, the social and 'objective' sides of free indirect style have dominated the scene: the 'truths' of the neo-classical narrator, the *doxa* of public opinion, the force of abstract ideas, the voice of small communities, of social classes, of collective oral myths . . . But around 1900 a different group of writers begins to experiment at the opposite end of the spectrum, that of the irreducibly singular. First comes a cluster of upper-class stylizations (James, Mann, Proust, Woolf . . .), where the deviation from social norms is often so slight that it may not even form a separate branch; then, more decisive, Joyce's generation unceremoniously drops all stylistic good manners, and pushes its field of observation well inside the secret, unconscious layers of psychic life. The 'objective' side of free indirect style does not quite disappear, if only because of the countless commonplaces that *Ulysses* inherits from *Bouvard and Pécuchet*: but Joyce reverses their function, and subordinates them to the centrifugal, idiosyncratic drift of Bloom's associations. It's the same double register, and the same final outcome, as that of *Crime and Punishment*: just as, there, the third person of free indirect style had approached the second person of dialogism, but had been finally ousted by it—so, in *Ulysses*, the third person is constantly drifting towards, but also yielding to the *first* person of Joyce's chosen technique, the stream of consciousness.[25] Here, too, cultural 'interbreeding' encountered a barrier that could not be passed.

[25] 'He looked down at the boots he had blacked and polished. She had outlived him. Lost her husband. More dead for her than for me. One must outlive the other. Wise men say. There are more women than men in the world. Condole with her. Your terrible loss. I hope you'll soon follow him. For hindu widows only. She would marry another. Him? No. Yet who knows after.' James Joyce, *Ulysses*, ch. 6.

In the final branching of the tree—Latin American 'dictator novels'—the fluctuation between third and first person is still there, but its direction has been reversed: in place of a third-person narrative modulating into a first-person monologue, we see the dictator's attempt to objectify his private (and pathological) self into the monumental poses of a public persona. 'My dynasty begins and ends in me, in I-HE,' writes Augusto Roa Bastos in *I the Supreme*; and towards the end of the book:

> HE, erect, with his usual brio, the sovereign power of his first day. One hand behind him, the other tucked in the lapel of his frock coat . . . I is HE, definitively, I-HE-SUPREME. Immemorial. Imperishable.[26]

In Roa Bastos's novel, as in Carpentier's *Reasons of State* and García Márquez's *General in his Labyrinth*—the other two dictator novels of 1974, a year after the *putsch* against Allende in Chile—the 'I' of El Supremo still largely overshadows his 'HE', thus confining free indirect style to quite a limited role. But with Mario Vargas Llosa the technique moves into the foreground, and realizes its full political potential: by presenting the mind of the dictator 'unmediated by any judging point of view'—to repeat Ann Banfield's limpid definition of free indirect style[27]—Vargas Llosa endows the putrid substratum of political terror with an unforgettably sinister matter-of-factness:

> Had the United States had a more sincere friend than him, in the past thirty-one years? What government had given them greater support in the UN? Which was the first to declare war on Germany and Japan? Who gave the biggest bribes to representatives, senators, governors, mayors, lawyers and reporters in the United States? His reward: economic sanctions by the OAS to make that nigger Rómulo Betancourt happy, to keep sucking at the tit of the Venezuelan oil. If Johnny Abbes had handled things better and the bomb had blown off the head of that faggot Rómulo, there

[26] Roa Bastos, *I the Supreme*, Normal, IL 2000, pp. 123, 419.
[27] Ann Banfield, *Unspeakable Sentences*, Boston 1982, p. 97.

wouldn't be any sanctions and the asshole gringos wouldn't be handing
him bullshit about sovereignty, democracy, and human rights.[28]

VII

From the abode of noise and impropriety, where nobody was in
their right place, to the asshole gringos handing him bullshit about
sovereignty, democracy, and human rights. This is what comparative literature could be, if it took itself seriously as *world literature*,
on the one hand, and as *comparative morphology*, on the other. Take
a form, follow it from space to space, and study the reasons for its
transformations: the 'opportunistic, hence unpredictable' reasons of
evolution, in Ernst Mayr's words.[29] And of course the multiplicity of
spaces is the great challenge, and the curse, almost, of comparative
literature: but it is also its peculiar strength, because it is only in such
a wide, non-homogeneous geography that some fundamental prin-
ciples of cultural history become manifest. As, here, the dependence
of morphological novelty on spatial discontinuity: 'allopatric speciation', to quote Ernst Mayr one more time: a new species (or at any
rate a new formal arrangement), arising when a population migrates
into a new homeland, and must quickly change in order to survive.
Just like free indirect style when it moves into Petersburg, Aci Trezza,
Dublin, Ciudad Trujillo . . .

Spatial discontinuity boosting morphological divergence. It's a situation that reminds me of Gide's reflections on the form of the novel at
the time he was writing *The Counterfeiters*: granted that the novel is a
slice of life, he muses, why should we always slice 'in the direction of
length', emphasizing the passage of time? why not slice *in the direction of width*, and of the multiplicity of simultaneous events? Length,

---

[28] Vargas Llosa, *The Feast of the Goat*, ch. 2.
[29] Mayr, *Toward a New Philosophy of Biology*, p. 458.

plus width: this is how a tree signifies. And you look at figure 33, or at the others before it, and cannot help but wonder: which is the most significant axis, here—the vertical, or the horizontal? Diachronic succession, or synchronic drifting apart? This perceptual uncertainty between time and (morpho-)space—this impossibility, in fact, of really 'seeing' them both at once—is the sign of a new conception of literary history, in which literature moves forwards *and sideways* at once; often, more sideways than forwards. Like Shklovsky's great metaphor for art, the knight's move at chess.

VIII

Three chapters; three models; three distinct 'sections' of the literary field. First, the system of novelistic genres as a whole; then, 'the road from birth to death' of a specific chronotope; and now, the micro-level of stylistic mutations. But despite the differences of scale, some aspects of the argument remain constant. First of all, a somewhat pragmatic view of theoretical knowledge. 'Theories are nets', wrote Novalis, 'and only he who casts will catch'. Yes, theories are nets, and we should evaluate them, not as ends in themselves, but for how they *concretely change the way we work*: for how they allow us to enlarge the literary field, and re-design it in a better way, replacing the old, useless distinctions (high and low; canon and archive; this or that national literature . . .) with new temporal, spatial, and morphological distinctions.

In the second place, the models I have presented also share a clear preference for explanation over interpretation; or perhaps, better, for the explanation of general structures over the interpretation of individual texts. This is of course a major issue in its own right; but for now, let me at least say that the point, here, was not a new reading of *Waverley*, or *Black Forest Village Stories*, or *I Malavoglia*, but the definition of those larger patterns that are their necessary preconditions:

the temporal cycles that determine the rise and fall of literary genres; the circular patterns of old village culture; the cluster of possibilities (and constraints) within which free indirect style accomplished its various symbolic tasks.

Were I to name a common denominator for all these attempts, I would probably choose: *a materialist conception of form.* An echo of the Marxist problematic of the 1960s and 70s? Yes and no. Yes, because the great idea of that critical season—form as the most profoundly social aspect of literature: *form as force,* as I put it in the close to my previous chapter—remains for me as valid as ever. And no, because I no longer believe that a single explanatory framework may account for the many levels of literary production and their multiple links with the larger social system: whence a certain conceptual eclecticism of these pages, and the tentative nature of many of the examples. Much remains to be done, of course, on the compatibility of the various models, and the explanatory hierarchy to be established among them. But right now, opening new conceptual possibilities seemed more important than justifying them in every detail.

Alberto Piazza

Evolution at Close Range

I.   I read the last chapter of this book first, because its title and author aroused my interest. That title 'Trees', and the second figure (no. 29) that appears in it concern me professionally, as I have devoted many years of my life to the analysis of evolutionary trees drawn from the biological data of human populations. The construction of that figure is based on such analyses. I have been able to devote less time to Franco Moretti's other writings; but *The Way of the World* and *Atlas of the European Novel* had earlier struck me by their ambition to tell the 'stories' of literary structures, or the evolution over time and space of cultural traits considered not in their singularity, but their complexity. An evolution, in other words, 'viewed from afar', analogous at least in certain respects to that which I have taught and practised in my study of genetics. Curiosity then prompted me to read the other two chapters of this triptych, and to offer some general reflections to its readers. What follows is an attempt to lay these out as a contribution to an interdisciplinary discussion, in the conviction that literary writing can be construed as a system that is not bound by the particular instruments it has itself created, and is therefore capable of metabolizing metaphors and ambiguities belonging to several systems of knowledge. I will add that the system of scientific knowledge, especially that of modern molecular biology, is paradoxically very well suited to such a metabolizing function: let me just point out how, in technical language, we commonly speak of the 'translation' and 'transcription' of DNA.

Biological evolution in a literary metaphor

2.   Biological evolution is based on the chemical structure of DNA, which is the biological memory of all beings, human or otherwise. Let us recall Genesis, Chapter 2:

18. And the Lord said, It is not good that the man should be alone: I will make him an help meet for him.

19. And out of the ground the Lord God formed every beast of the field, and every fowl of the air; and brought them unto Adam to see what he would call them: and whatsoever Adam called every living creature, that was the name thereof.

20. And Adam gave names to all cattle, and to the fowl of the air, and to every beast of the field; but for Adam there was not found an help meet for him.

21. And the Lord God caused a deep sleep to fall upon Adam, and he slept: and he took one of his ribs, and closed up the flesh instead thereof;

22. And the rib, which the Lord God had taken from man, made he a woman, and brought her unto the man.

We may deduce that the earliest way of possessing an object was to give it a name bearing as much information as possible: without information there is no possession of life. Yet for the object to enter, relate to and cooperate with us, in other words to be 'convivial', it is not enough to give it a name. There must be a mechanism of 'transcription' (the rib) that transmits the information from one organism to another, perhaps with some slight modification. The mechanism of sexual recombination (the exchange of chromosomes between man and woman) is one of the most effective among the many in which nature abounds. The literary metaphor of the rib (consciously or not) offers an elegant introduction to the concept of the transmission of information: we know today that DNA sequences are chains of chemical molecules, whose function is to contain the information that regulates the life of each of our cells, and to transmit it from one generation to the next, with changes that may be minimal but are very important for evolution.

3. For information to be transmitted accurately, without errors, a code is required. Linguistic codes and DNA codes, names and genes, present certain analogies in their rules of transmission: mutation, selection, drift are common to them. Both codes are ambiguous, redundant and degenerative. The presence of many names, of a lot of information, makes discrimination essential. What is needed, in other words, is a mechanism that ensures a sufficient but not unlimited variability of significations: thus in the human genome there are some 30-50,000 genes (that is, units of information), about the same number as there are words in Italian.

4. Information that is codified becomes organized in a structure. The structure evolves over time: the text therefore requires a context. Writing recalls the text from the context, constituting its memory. In the case of DNA, we know the alphabet, and we also know the text (the sequence of the human genome discovered in the last few years), but its meaning remains largely unknown, and constitutes the challenge of the years to come (the 'post-genome'—in a literary metaphor, 'post-modern'— years). Its writing is thus for the moment unreproducible, but it is endowed with a very long and precise memory (the so-called 'molecular clock').

In the case of the literary text, its function changes over time, often constituting a memory of the context more than of itself. In his book *In the Vineyard of the Text. Hugh's Didascalicon*, Ivan Illich comments on the *Didascalicon* of the theologian and mystic Ugo di San Vittore, written around 1128. Ugo di San Vittore testified to a transformation of the ancient art of memorizing a monastic manuscript that was intended to be read aloud, to the new art of a book designed to serve history. To read is tantamount to recreating the historical tissue in the heart of the reader. A text, then, that is memory of the past and presage of future transformations of its context.

5.   In the biological world of DNA, reading and writing belong to two different but complementary systems. The fact that DNA has the shape of a double and not a single helix obeys the rule that the reading of DNA must be faithfully transcribed, without errors. Much of the energy of our cells is devoted to correcting possible errors of transcription: only a minimal number of these are 'fortunate' errors, in the sense that they can be favourable rather than harmful to our organism, and hence in a broad sense to our species. Still, the presence of the context has induced in us humans—being typically cultural animals—an evolution of the nervous systems that we are currently discovering with astonishment and wonder. The technique of functional magnetic resonance allows us to visualize the activation of the circuits in the brain that preside over the most variegated cognitive paths. Here I would like to mention just one, fascinating field of research into our system of reading. If an individual is asked to read a word, and then the same individual is read the word at a moment when he or she no longer remembers it, a comparison of the two images captured by magnetic resonance reveals that quite distinct areas of the brain are activated. Without entering into the particulars of the functional anatomy implied in the reading and hearing of the same words, let us just emphasise

once more the importance of the context: an identical meaning is perceived by two distinct cognitive systems according to the way in which it is transmitted. Ambiguity, allusion, redundance, often vilified as means of cultural impoverishment, are vindicated as forms that not only belong to the literary field, but intervene in that subtle play which begins with the pre-lexical and pre-semantic representation of a text perceived as a picture, and ends in the context-dependent working-out of their meaning.

6. The role of variability in the memory of the past and the construction of the present is fundamental for the evolution of our species: the search for the ways in which this variability is generated in nature was for a long time the major stumbling-block for Darwin, who by a strange quirk of fate never learnt of the revolutionary work of Mendel.

In his *Way of the World*, Franco Moretti proposes the very interesting idea that even literary genres cannot survive without cultural variety. The genre of the *Bildungsroman*, he shows, was born in Europe after the French Revolution in response to a precise social need: mediation of the conflicting demands of freedom and stability. The narration of youth allows this dilemma to be symbolically transcended: if as a mature man I narrate my youth, I depict the indeterminacy of my past in the determinate, stable voice of the adult I have become. In the mediation of a tension with a distension, however, the narrative register creates an equilibrium that is the prelude to a loss of the original creative tension, and thus to the progressive extinction of the genre. But in the very different, and ethnically more heterogeneous setting of the United States, a *Bildungsroman* was reborn in which youth itself narrated its own moral education, in Salinger's *Catcher in the Rye*. Moretti suggests that the cultural variability of the American context allowed the transplant of a literary form that had exhausted its social function in Europe.

Biological evolution (very briefly)

7. Recognizing the role biological variability plays in the reconstruction of the memory of our (biological) past requires ways to visualize and elaborate data at our disposal on a geographical basis. To this end, let us consider a gene (a segment of DNA possessed of a specific, ascertainable biological function); and for each gene let us analyse its identifiable variants, or *alleles*. The percentage of individuals who carry a given allele may vary (very widely) from one geographical locality to another. If we can verify the presence or absence of that allele in a sufficient number of individuals living in a circumscribed and uniform geographical area, we can draw maps whose isolines will join all the points with the same proportion of alleles.

   The geographical distribution of such genetic frequencies can yield indications and instruments of measurement of the greatest interest for the study of the evolutionary mechanisms that generate genetic differences between human populations. But their interpretation involves quite complex problems. When two human populations are genetically similar, the resemblance may be the result of a common historical origin, but it can also be due to their settlement in similar physical (for example, climatic) environments. Nor should we forget that styles of life and cultural attitudes of an analogous nature (for example, dietary regimes) can favour the increase or decrease to the point of extinction of certain genes.

8. Why do genes (and hence their frequencies) vary over time and space? They do so because the DNA sequences of which they are composed can change by accident. Such change, or *mutation*,

occurs very rarely, and when it happens, it persists equally rarely in a given population in the long run. Most of the genes of which we have knowledge undergo a mutation about every million generations. From an evolutionary point of view, the mechanism of mutation is very important because it introduces innovations; but since our species of *Homo sapiens* has existed only for some thousands of generations, it is very improbable that mutations exclusive to our species have contributed significantly to the differences that make one population, or one individual, genetically distinct from another. We should rather think of different versions of the same genes that pre-existed the origin of our species, and over time have acquired a different incidence in different populations.

The evolutionary mechanism capable of changing the genetic structure of a population most swiftly is *natural selection*, which favours the genetic types best adapted for survival to sexual maturity, or with a higher fertility. Natural selection, whose action is continuous over time, having to eliminate mutations that are injurious in a given habitat, is the mechanism that adapts a population to the environment that surrounds it, be this tropical, temperate or arctic. The speed of this adaptive process can be quantified and predicted on the basis of the relative distribution of each genetic type transmitted from one generation to the next.

Another evolutionary mechanism is *random genetic drift*. It is the result of the fact that each new generation is produced by a random sample of the genes present in the preceding generation. Take the example of the founders of a new colony on a remote island, with few contacts with the outside world. If by pure chance these founders lack a gene, that gene will disappear from the entire population of the island. Since each generation can be considered a population sample founding the next generation, the smaller a given population and the greater its isolation, the wider may be the fluctuations of the frequency of a gene from one generation to the next. Unlike natural selection which favours or penalizes single genes, random genetic drift influences all genes in the same way, altering the frequency of each.

Migration, the mechanism that unites two physically and genetically separate populations, also acts simultaneously on all genes, but more consistently than random genetic drift. Individuals of population A who emigrate to population B modify the genetic frequencies of population B, rendering it more like population A, with all the genetic frequencies changing in the same direction.

Of these evolutionary mechanisms, genetic drift is the only one consistent with a phylogenetic representation constructed as a *tree* of evolution—that is, a series of successive separations of population. A tree offers a good image of the evolution of human populations only when the population depicted on each branch of the tree evolves (that is, changes its genetic frequencies) independently of the changes occurring in the populations on the other branches. There is a good statistical correspondence between the genetic data and some evolutionary trees of human differentiation: one that is all the better when the populations in question are geographically and genetically distant from each other—which is what we would expect, given that the more distant the populations are from each other, the less can their evolutions correlate after their separation. If, on the other hand, we look at European populations, among whom well-known pre-historic and historic migrations have led to mixtures that make independent changes among them highly improbable, the image of a tree is not a good representation of evolution. Another result of the elaboration of real data is that the branches representing the evolution of various populations are of different lengths, as if the pace of change of each population were measured by clocks of different speeds. This reflects the fact that genetic drift produces a greater change in small and isolated populations, while migration can slow down such change by 'mixing' the genes of populations in the same territory, thus reducing the differences induced by genetic drift. In other words, the rates of evolutionary change can vary from population to population: a population that has undergone many migrations (and is therefore very diverse internally but probably less distinct from other populations) evolves less rapidly—is perched on a shorter branch of the tree—than a population that is isolated (hence rather uniform internally but probably more distinct from other populations). For the historical reasons already adduced, European populations are among those that show a slower rate of evolution than others, and for this reason too it could be misleading to reconstruct their evolution over time in the simple form of a tree.

Evolution of literary form

9. To find out at what point a biological metaphor ceases to be such, and becomes an appropriate research instrument for the history of literary forms, we need to see if the evolutionary mechanisms that produce biological changes—mutations, natural selection, genetic drift and migration—have their counterparts in those active on literary forms. Let me venture some hypotheses.

In the first place, the evolutionary mechanisms in the biology and culture of our species manifest interesting correspondences. If we take language as a cultural phenomenon *par excellence*, of the four mechanisms that govern our genetic change, we can say that: *migration* influences genes and languages in the same way; *selection* operates in both fields—natural selection favouring the phenotype best adapted to survive, and cultural selection the reciprocal lexical and phonetic intelligibility of language; *mutation* and *linguistic innovation* perform the same function— generating changes which, after occurring by chance in single individuals, are then adopted by other individuals.

Turning more specifically from language to literary form, *migration* is certainly a factor of change. *Graphs, Maps, Trees* does not tell us how far translation of the same novel into different languages may alter the reception and success of a literary genre in the country where it is translated, but Moretti's findings in the third chapter of *Atlas of the European Novel*, on literary diffusion and the correlation between literary models and geographical space, suggest an important role for migration, not of people but of 'forms', at least in Europe. Just as *natural selection* in biology denotes the selection of the biological type that best survives in the given environment, so there is no doubt that some literary forms have more success than others and survive longer thanks to multiple cultural and economic factors of which the graphs in the first chapter of this book (for example, figures 3 to 10) furnish ample and valuable illustration. There is no need to spend many words on *mutation*, which, by analogy with the biological mechanism, could supply the factors capable of originating a new literary form: as in biology (where mutations of DNA are caused by the most varied agents), such factors are presumably quite diverse, but it is less important to identify their exact nature than to be sure of their existence. Figure 1 of 'Graphs' seems more than convincing on this score. What remains to establish is the existence of an evolutionary mechanism analogous to *random genetic drift*, an extremely delicate task because—as I have explained above—the significance of evolutionary trees in biology depends in large measure on the presence or absence of this mechanism.

10. A genetic trait can differ profoundly from a cultural typology not only in the evolutionary mechanisms that generate variability, but also in the mechanism whereby such variability is transmitted. While in biology the transmission of information can occur only from parent to child, cultural transmission can make use of other mechanisms. According to the schema proposed by Cavalli-Sforza and Feldman in their *Cultural Transmission and Evolution. A Quantitative Approach* (Princeton 1981), there are four possible modes of relation between subject and object in the transmission of information:

A) *From parent to child (vertical)*. This is the mechanism that diffuses biological information, working slowly but selected to preserve inter-individual variability.

B) *From one individual to another (horizontal)*. This is a mechanism analogous to contagion in an epidemic, where information spreads rapidly.

C) *From one to several individuals* (for example, from a teacher to pupils or a leader to followers). This is the most effective mechanism for the diffusion of an innovation in a social group.

D) *From several individuals to a single individual*. This is the mechanism of social pressure: it generally thwarts the diffusion of an innovation.

What is the mechanism of transmission most relevant to literary genres? Even if mechanism A played a pre-eminent role in the past, and explains those links between genes and languages that we can still recognize today, it is clear that the diffusion of a literary genre cannot dispense with a market that favours mechanism C. The family, which has hitherto ensured the transmission not only of genes but of culture, gives way to the figure of the *leader*— the novelist, if the genre in question is the novel: the transmission of information runs from the single individual to several individuals. The evolutionary mechanism known as *genetic drift* acquires in this context especial relevance. As explained, in genetics drift is the phenomenon whereby the smaller a population, the more frequently genes display only one variant. This is something we readily observe in surnames, which can be considered comparable to the genes to be found in the male chromosome Y: in a country with few inhabitants the number of identical surnames tends to increase, reaching 100 per cent if the population is composed of just a single individual. In evolutionary terms, drift reduces the genetic diversity of the population, and therewith its adaptive capacity.

Now the cultural mechanism of transmission *from one to several individuals* represents the most extreme case of such drift: it is as if a single individual transmitted his genes to an entire population, thus reducing and progressively extinguishing genetic diversity. In other words: cultural drift could diffuse cultural information significantly faster, but at the price of reducing it. Moretti's data suggest that the evolution of literary forms has been possible till now, or till yesterday, because of their high capacity for innovation, illustrated in figure 9 of 'Graphs', plotting the English novel from 1740 to 1900. An evolutionary equilibrium between genetic drift, which tends towards homogeneity (and so non-evolution), and mutation, which tends towards innovation, is the condition—well studied at a theoretical level—of hereditary pathologies in isolated populations. Biological reality, as always, is more complex, because natural selection also comes into play if the hereditary pathology is lethal (or less dramatically but more rarely, if treatment exists for it), with results that depend on the relative weight of the three factors at work. It is easy to imagine that literary genres also undergo the influence of factors of cultural selection, which have to be studied in the social-historical context (see, for example, the problem of change in literary publics posed by the appearance and disappearance at regular intervals of the English novelistic genres). The challenge here is to distinguish between the various layers of the term 'environment', which students of biological evolution, as of other disciplines, are fond of using with casual vagueness. A still more radical challenge, putting in question the formulation of quantitative models themselves, is posed by the possibly non-linear nature of such factors: the existence of cyclical patterns of behaviour, for instance, like those revealed in figures 7 and 8 on the hegemonic forms of the English novel in the 18–19th centuries, is always the sign—also in biology—of the presence of non-linear phenomena. The fact, then, that non-linear phenomena are the norm and not the exception (one need only think of the simple phenomenon of growth in any discipline) constitutes one of the major limits to the development of quantitative models in every field of knowledge today.

Trees

11. Trees in general, such as those to be found in figures 28 and 29, are representations composed of a series of successive bifurcations, that depict with maximum economy all the reciprocal 'distances'—or overall diversification—between whatever objects are in question. For example the first tree (figure 28), which may not be easy to read for those viewing such a representation for the first time, illustrates a trait that 'diverges' over time—that is, changes in a succession of variants (in the figure, from bottom to top), of which only some persist through all the diversifications made possible by natural selection to date (represented in the figure by the horizontal line higher up). This is a tree which represents the divergence of a trait over time, or the distance of the trait in question from the moment of its initial observation to that of its final observation after a certain lapse of time. To make the representation clearer, let us suppose the trait is a gene, and that this gene is the sequence of DNA made up of

five elements which I designate AATTC (the real name to which the letters refer is irrelevant). The gene evolves over time—that is, changes. To represent this change in the form of a tree, I must define both a point of departure (the 'root' of the tree) and a line that joins the root to a point representing the moment at which the first change happens, which we may imagine as altering the third element from T to G. A mutation has occurred in the gene AATTC, which becomes the gene AAGTC. From now on the two genes AATTC and AAGTC coexist, and their coexistence is represented by a bifurcation of the tree. Such a point (or time) of bifurcation is called a 'node' of the tree. Every successive episode of diversification can be represented analogously by a node at which a bifurcation originates, and the tree as a whole becomes a succession of bifurcations, at the end of which (that is, at the extremity of the tree which will usually represent the present) we have as many genes that have mutated from the original in the root of the tree as there are bifurcations plus 1, unless some of these have become extinct through natural selection. The non-extinct genes which appear at the extremity of the tree are technically called its 'leaves'. What I have just described is the 'phylogenetic tree' of the gene, in the sense that it depicts its evolutionary phylogenesis over time from an initial gene. The reality of the data available to us is, however, quite different. We know the genes that are present today (the leaves of the tree) and we want to infer, without knowing them, the various transitions that have led from the root to the current situation. The phylogenetic tree is thus 'reconstructed' by a process of retrospective inference, based on an evolutionary model. For example, it is generally assumed that evolution proceeds at the same rate of change along all branches of the tree; that changes from one node to another are the least possible; that natural selection does not operate; that we cannot find the same change simultaneously in different branches of the tree. It is very important to understand that a tree-like structure (technically a 'topology') cannot reflect the phylogenesis of the object in question if its evolutionary history is not consistent with the assumptions on which the process of inference is based. Awareness of this is all the more important today, when intensive and often heedless use of computers is capable of generating trees of any aggregate of objects whose reciprocal distance is known. With most of the algorithms now in use, the tree will merely reproduce a topology in which the objects closest to one another will be separated by a lesser number of nodes, and those more distant from each other by a larger number; but it can have no pretension to be a phylogenetic description if the algorithm employed is not congruent with a reasonable model of evolution, whose mechanisms have been explicitly formulated.

12.   The tree represented in figure 29 differs from figure 28. Its leaves are not different variants of the same trait or gene, but different linguistic populations or families, distributed across the five continents. What are the relations between the two types of tree and what assumptions are required for testing the phylogenetic validity of the evolutionary tree of human linguistic populations or families? We need to remember that each individual in our species has about 30–50,000 genes, and that every population is composed of many individuals, whose history we assume to be common, at least as regards geographical settlement. Since each individual differs from the next by about two per thousand (or 0.2%) of his or her DNA, it is reasonable to think that the evolution over time of a gene, or an individual, or a population, will have different rates of changes, and thus different evolutionary trees, that will certainly be correlated but in an unpredictable way. The only certain relationship is that bifurcations in the tree of populations must occur later than bifurcations in the genes of the individuals who compose them: this temporal lag is due to the fact that the individuals of one population differ from those of another by cumulative mutations within many genes and not

a single gene. Still, this important distinction between trees of genes and trees of populations is of little interest if the leaves in question are cultural traits like literary genres. More interesting, however, are two properties of the phylogenetic trees drawn from the study of biological evolution:

A) If the tree is used to infer the times at which bifurcation occurred, the changes through all the branches, from root to leaves, it is necessary for the changes of the branches, from root to leaves, to occur at a constant speed. This is realistic enough in trees of genes, in so far as single genes vary over time at a roughly constant rate. But it is not realistic in trees of populations, where the variability of genes and individuals is cumulative, and the demography of each population can speed up or slow down change. In other words, here every branch has its own specific rate of variation.

B) A real tree of life would foresee not only bifurcations, but trifurcations, quadrifurcations etc, and still more important, the possibility that once diversified, two or more populations can join together in a reticular weave where genes and cultures not only diverge but converge, as depicted in Kroeber's tree of culture reproduced in figure 32. That the tree in figure 29 is a fairly realistic representation of the evolution of human populations and languages depends on the fact that the populations are geographically distant and distinct from one another, and that the number of mutual 'borrowings' between linguistic 'families' is reasonably small. If one were to apply the same tree structure to European populations, it would become evident that the model of successive bifurcations is incomplete, since the network of migrations between different countries would create a reticular structure that could not be confined to tree-like form. From a practical standpoint, however, the development of reticular models is a much more complex, not to say currently impossible, task; so for the moment we must content ourselves with testing the hypothesis that the data can be explained with the model of a tree, in the knowledge that if this hypothesis is not statistically proven, the alternative hypothesis of a reticular structure is the more probable.

13. These methodological remarks make possible a specific comment on the trees presented in the third chapter of this book. Figure 30 represents the phylogenesis of the English detective story, where clues constitute the morphological trait (in biology we would speak of a 'phenotype') that changes over time. This is a tree of the type that tracks changes in a gene and it is easy to reconstruct a biological image of it. Corresponding to each mutation, the nodes of the tree, are enumerated the populations (or individuals) in which the mutant gene is to be found. From a study of the distribution of the populations or individuals associated with each node—that is, the mutation which the node represents—we can infer the 'adaptive' value of the mutation for the individual or the population, in other words whether or not the mutation has been 'chosen' by natural selection to confer an advantage (which is then its presence) or a disadvantage (its absence) on the individual or population. In the tree of clues and the tree of the gene the problem lies not in their topology but, as Moretti himself acknowledges, in the selection and completeness of the clues (mutations) taken into consideration. In order to avoid a circular argument, caution would also suggest that the selection of detective stories and that of clues should be not only as complete as possible, but also independent of each other.

The last tree offered and analysed in this book depicts the evolution from 1800 till today of the narrative technique known as 'free indirect style'. It is reproduced in figure 33. In this bold experiment of comparative morphology, the idea we have noted in Moretti's account of the *Bildungsroman* returns: that there exists a relation between spatial discontinuity and morphological innovation. This is one of the most stimulating findings of *Graphs, Maps, Trees*. In Moretti's words, 'a new species (or at any rate a new formal arrangement), arising when a population migrates into a new homeland, and must quickly change in order to survive. Just like free indirect style when it moves into Petersburg, Aci Trezza, Dublin, Ciudad Trujillo . . .'. We are dealing, in a literary metaphor, with that 'allopatric speciation' which Ernst Mayr postulated in the 1940s and 50s to account for the birth of different species of birds in the same habitat by exclusive effect of geographical distance and lack of genetic exchange. The adoption of a similar model for new stylistic variants, or cultural traits, presupposes that the various branches of the tree cannot exchange information: in the case of free indirect style under consideration, this condition is secured by linguistic discontinuities, but in other applications it would have to be established case by case.

Epilogue

14. The stimuli offered by this book of Franco Moretti's are many and fascinating, and my remarks are intended as a tribute to them from one who is not a practitioner of the same field, but would like to respond to its challenge. In that spirit, let me end with a reflection. Phylogenetic trees representing biological evolution presuppose an absence and a presence: absence of the effects of natural selection and presence of mutation, migration and random genetic drift. That is not because natural selection is held to be of little weight, but because it can operate in many different ways and its effect on the branches of the tree may be to make them either diverge or converge. In so ambiguous and unpredictable a situation, it is better to assume that natural selection has no effect, and then to confirm or falsify this hypothesis statistically. By contrast in all the trees representing the evolution of different literary forms in Moretti's book, cultural selection—the survival or extinction of one form rather than another—is the principal operator. This different approach probably reflects different questions. The student of biological evolution is especially interested in the root of the tree (the time

it originated). For inferring this origin, direct consideration of natural selection is an encumbrance to be avoided, by studying the effect of many genes whose relative weights can be ignored because divergences and convergences cancel each other out. The student of literary evolution, on the other hand, is interested not so much in the root of the tree (because it is situated in a known historical epoch) as in its trajectory, or metamorphoses. This is an interest much closer to study of the evolution of a gene, the particular nature of whose mutations, and the filter operated by natural selection, one wants to understand. It is only today, when we know the human genome and can deploy very powerful technologies of molecular biology, that the possibility of retracing the history of all the mutations of a gene across its (and our) evolution has ceased to be illusory. In their wide-open challenge, I have found in Moretti's conjectures an incentive to refine the means of reading our evolution. I would be happy if it were so for other readers too.

Index

Printed in the United States
by Baker & Taylor Publisher Services